# Professionalizing Second Language Writing

SECOND LANGUAGE WRITING
Series Editor: Paul Kei Matsuda

Second language writing emerged in the late twentieth century as an interdisciplinary field of inquiry, and an increasing number of researchers from various related fields—including applied linguistics, communication, composition studies, and education—have come to identify themselves as second language writing specialists. The Second Language Writing series aims to facilitate the advancement of knowledge in the field of second language writing by publishing scholarly and research-based monographs and edited collections that provide significant new insights into central topics and issues in the field.

## BOOKS IN THE SERIES

*The Politics of Second Language Writing: In Search of the Promised Land*, edited by Paul Kei Matsuda, Christina Ortmeier-Hooper, and Xiaoye You (2006)
*Building Genre Knowledge* by Christine M. Tardy (2009)
*Practicing Theory in Second Language Writing*, edited by Tony Silva and Paul Kei Matsuda (2010)
*Foreign Language Writing Instruction: Principles and Practices*, edited by Tony Cimasko and Melinda Reichelt (2011)
*Scientific Writing in a Second Language* by David Ian Hanauer and Karen Englander (2013)
*Graduate Studies in Second Language Writing*, edited by Kyle McIntosh, Carolina Pelaez-Morales, and Tony Silva (2015)
*Professionalizing Second Language Writing*, edited by Paul Kei Matsuda, Sarah Elizabeth Snyder, and Katherine Daily O'Meara (2017)

# PROFESSIONALIZING SECOND LANGUAGE WRITING

Edited by

Paul Kei Matsuda, Sarah Elizabeth Snyder, and Katherine Daily O'Meara

Parlor Press
*Anderson, South Carolina*
www.parlorpress.com

Parlor Press LLC, Anderson, South Carolina, USA

© 2018 by Parlor Press
All rights reserved.
Printed in the United States of America
SAN: 254-8879

Library of Congress Cataloging-in-Publication Data

Names: Matsuda, Paul Kei, editor. | Snyder, Sarah Elizabeth, editor. | O'Meara, Katherine Daily, editor.
Title: Professionalizing second language writing / edited by Paul Kei Matsuda, Sarah Elizabeth Snyder, and Katherine Daily O'Meara.
Description: Anderson, South Carolina : Parlor Press, [2017] | Series: Second language writing | Includes bibliographical references and index.
Identifiers: LCCN 2017045799 (print) | LCCN 2017054890 (ebook) | ISBN 9781602359697 (pdf) | ISBN 9781602359703 (epub) | ISBN 9781602359710 (ibook) | ISBN 9781602359727 (mobi) | ISBN 9781602359673 (pbk. : alk. paper) | ISBN 9781602359680 (hardcover : alk. paper) | ISBN 9781602359710 (ibook)
Subjects: LCSH: Language and languages--Study and teaching (Higher) | Rhetoric--Study and teaching (Higher) | Academic writing--Study and teaching (Higher) | Report writing--Study and teaching (Higher) | Second language acquisition.
Classification: LCC P59.27 (ebook) | LCC P59.27 .P78 2017 (print) | DDC 418.0071/1--dc23
LC record available at https://lccn.loc.gov/2017045799

2 3 4 5

Second Language Writing
Series Editor: Paul Kei Matsuda

Cover design by Paul Kei Matsuda and David Blakesley
Printed on acid-free paper.

Parlor Press, LLC is an independent publisher of scholarly and trade titles in print and multimedia formats. This book is available in paper, cloth and eBook formats from Parlor Press on the World Wide Web at http://www.parlorpress.com or through online and brick-and-mortar bookstores. For submission information or to find out about Parlor Press publications, write to Parlor Press, 3015 Brackenberry Drive, Anderson, South Carolina, 29621, or email editor@parlorpress.com.

# Contents

Preface   *vii*

1 Representations of Professionalization in Second Language Writing: A View from the Flagship Journal   *3*
 *Christine M. Tardy*

2 Where It All Begins: Doctoral Studies as Professional Development in Second Language Writing   *21*
 *Dwight Atkinson*

3 Negotiating an Academic Position as an L2 Writing Specialist: The Case of a Second Language (L2) Writing Specialist in a Joint Appointment   *33*
 *Pisarn Bee Chamcharatsri*

4 An Early-Career Second Language Writing Scholar's Professional Development in Japan: Challenges and Issues   *44*
 *Atsushi Iida*

5 Emergent Professional Identities of an Early Career L2 Writing Scholar   *54*
 *Soo Hyon Kim*

6 Publishing as an Early Second Languague Writing Scholar: Developing an Academic Voice and Navigating Disciplinary Expectations   *66*
 *Todd Ruecker*

7 Working Toward Being a Tenured Writing Program Administrator   *80*
 *Tanita Saenkhum*

8 Fake It 'Til You Make It: The Imposter Phenomenon
   in Gendered Academia                                               90
   *Deborah Crusan*

**Contributors**                                                     *111*

**Index**                                                            *115*

**About the Editors**                                                *121*

# Preface

The field of second language writing has grown tremendously over the last two decades, and many teachers, scholars and administrators from various disciplinary perspectives and institutional contexts have come to identify themselves as second language writing specialists. While the disciplinary infrastructure has grown and opportunities for graduate education have expanded, and while there is a small but growing number of resources for graduate students (e.g., Casanave & Vandrick, 2003; McIntosh, Pelaez-Morales, & Silva, 2016), there is a dearth of resources for the professional development of L2 writing specialists who are transitioning from being a graduate student to becoming an early-career professional in various institutional contexts.

The goal of this volume is to bring together active second language writing specialists at various stages of professional development to discuss the nature of professionalization in the field and to share stories of their entry into the profession and various issues and challenges they faced in the process. In Chapter 1, Christine Tardy, one of the co-editors of the *Journal of Second Language Writing* and an accomplished researcher, discusses the professionalization of the field by examining the flagship journal for generational shifts in the development of the field. In Chapter 2, Dwight Atkinson, another eminent scholar in the field, discusses the professionalization process that takes place in the doctoral program, offering a perspective on the amount and intensity of effort required for successful professionalization.

The next six chapters provide insights into various issues, challenges, and learning experiences that early-career L2 writing professionals face. In Chapter 3, Pisarn Bee Chamcharatsr addresses the issues that translingual scholars sometimes face as they accept dual-appointment tenure-track positions. In Chapter 4, Atsushi Iida discusses the challenges of establishing himself as a productive member of the field while meeting the demands of teaching and service as a non-tenure-track faculty member. In Chapter 5, Soo Hyon Kim explores how the transdisciplinary nature of the field affects the experience of an early-career L2 writing specialist as she engaged in teaching, research and service activities. In Chapter 6, Todd Ruecker shares his experience of learning to write for publication in an interdisciplinary terrain, where different disciplinary expectations and practices intersect. Chapter 7 by Tanita Saenkhum describes the dilemma of an untenured faculty member specializing in L2 writing program administration, and how she negotiates the balance between establishing her professional career and her administrative role.

The volume concludes with an inspiring exploration of the Imposter Phenomenon that affects not only early-career professionals but also many senior members of the field. In Chapter 8, Deborah Crusan documents the extent to which the Imposter Phenomenon affects professionals, how it is also a gendered issue, and how she struggled through it.

Together these chapters provide insights that can help graduate students and early career professionals as they envision their future and cope with new issues and challenges in their own processes of professionalization.

# Professionalizing Second Language Writing

# 1 Representations of Professionalization in Second Language Writing: A View from the Flagship Journal

*Christine M. Tardy*

Admittedly, when I was first invited to contribute to a scholarly discussion of professionalization in second language writing, I panicked a bit, imagining what I could possibly offer to the conversation. I knew that those who had been in the field longer than I could offer first-hand reflections on the field's development, those with more experience working with doctoral students could provide insights into graduate students' professional paths, and those who were versed in historical research methodologies could provide richer and more systematic analyses of the field's trajectories than I. Simply put, I wasn't sure what perspective I might bring to the issue that might be of interest. After some thought, though, I realized that much of how I currently think about the field of second language writing (and I will use the term "field" here, in part to bypass discussions of our disciplinary status[1]) is bound to my very fortunate current positioning as a co-editor of the *Journal of Second Language Writing*, arguably our flagship journal. In occupying this vantage point since 2011, I have found myself increasingly aware of the role that the journal plays in defining and influencing conceptions of second language writing and also in the field's professionalization.

Obviously the *JSLW* is only one site from which to view professionalization, but it offers a rich perspective. We find constructions of "the field" through the *JSLW*'s mission and scope, manuscript submissions and published papers, peer reviews, editorial decisions, special issue topics, annotated bibliographies, the disciplinary dialogues sections, the editorial board members, the editors, and even the publisher—a global company that owns over 2,000 journals, mostly in scientific fields. Thanks in large part to the founding editors, Ilona Leki and Tony Silva, the journal has provided an important venue for a growing sense of a community with specialized knowledge and a professional identity. In this chapter, then, I share a perspective on professionalization that is situated in various components of the *JSLW*. I begin, though, by building a framework for my discussion that attempts to understand the term professionalization as it relates to the development of a field and the related process of disciplinarity.

## PROFESSIONALIZATION AND DISCIPLINARY DEVELOPMENT

I don't want to conflate the processes of professionalization and disciplinarity entirely, but I also think it is useful to understand the two as related. Both are social processes that shape the professional identity of a group. Krishnan (2009) takes a sociological perspective on professionalization, defining it as:

> a social process through which an activity becomes a means for people to make a living. A professional is someone who can carry out a certain activity with a higher level of skill and knowledge than an amateur and someone who is paid for it sufficiently to base their own livelihood on that activity. (pp. 26–27)

By characterizing professionalization as social, Krishnan highlights implicitly that a professional is granted such recognition by others in society and that "professional" skills are those that have garnered some market value.

Social theorist Max Weber (1968) described professionalization as an evolutionary process, also deeply embedded in social values and practices. Professions don't begin as professions; rather, groups with shared practices gradually become recognized as the people who do those things. As they are granted that role, they are also given the time to devote to it, allowing them to think about it deeply, increasing their knowledge and honing their skills, and creating a vested interest in making their work valuable to others—in other words, creating capital around what they do. As they become more specialized, they develop more abstract and complex ways of thinking about their area of work; this usually requires specialized jargon and, eventually, specialized theories and practices.

In one such application of Weber's ideas to modern professions, Ritzer (1975) identified several defining features of a profession:

- Power
- Doctrine or general systematic knowledge
- Rational training
- Vocational qualifications
- Specialization
- A full-time occupation
- Existence of a clientele
- Salaries, promotions, professional duties, and a professional culture

A field like medicine or law would seem to obviously have these characteristics of a profession, but what about second language writing? Some of these characteristics seem questionable, with a great many teachers of second language writing lacking specialized qualifications or a full-time occupation, but we do have training in the form of MA and PhD programs in areas like TESOL, applied linguistics, and writing studies, and there is most certainly a clientele in both English-dominant and English as an additional language (EAL) countries.

In a 1990 *College English* article, Ohmann's (1990) description of professions also draws attention to their potentially *contentious* nature. Professions are, in his words:

> . . . socially made categories, and processes. A group that is doing a particular kind of work organizes itself in a professional association; appropriates, shares, and develops a body of knowledge as its own; discredits other practitioners performing similar work; establishes definite routes of admission, including but not limited to academic study; controls access; and gets recognition as the only group allowed to perform that kind of work, ideally with state power backing its monopoly. The process doesn't end there. Every constituted profession must continue to defend its rights and its borders. (p. 250)

Ohman's description may be particularly apt for academic professions and disciplines, where we often see overlaps and struggles among groups with similar interests and skills but perhaps competing histories, values, and practices. As a field lying betwixt and between several fields of knowledge—second language acquisition (SLA), discourse analysis, education, composition studies—second language writing is no stranger to such struggles.

Looking at disciplinary development, rather than professionalization, Shneider (2009), a biomedical researcher, outlines a four-stage model that characterizes both the nature of the research *and* the researchers at each stage of development. His description of disciplinary evolution emphasizes a move toward increasing specialization and rigor, accompanied by development of particular research techniques and topics of inquiry. Although this model aims to describe the evolution of scientific knowledge and disciplines, it serves as a useful starting point for looking at our own field.

Drawing on these models and definitions, we might represent the processes of professionalization and disciplinarity as roughly parallel but with overlapping and also at times distinct features, as demonstrated in Figure 1. As a group professionalizes, we would expect to see increasingly abstract and complex ways of thinking, increased jargon used to capture these ways of thinking, development of specialized training and qualifications, the development of a body of general or systematic knowledge, and the existence of a professional culture. Development of a discipline might, similarly, be characterized by the establishment of topics of study, research methodologies, specialized language and theories, and increased sophistication of research. The definitions I have drawn on so far emphasize the social processes involved in professionalization and disciplinarity, but I think it is also fair—and useful—to characterize them as *discursively constructed* processes. Such construction occurs in professional sites such as conferences, professional organizations, and through journals, because these are the places in which community members talk about, debate, and represent "the field." Taking *JSLW* as a discursive space of great relevance to the field of second language writing, then, I consider in this chapter how these processes of professionalization and disciplinarity might be reflected in and constructed through the flagship journal.

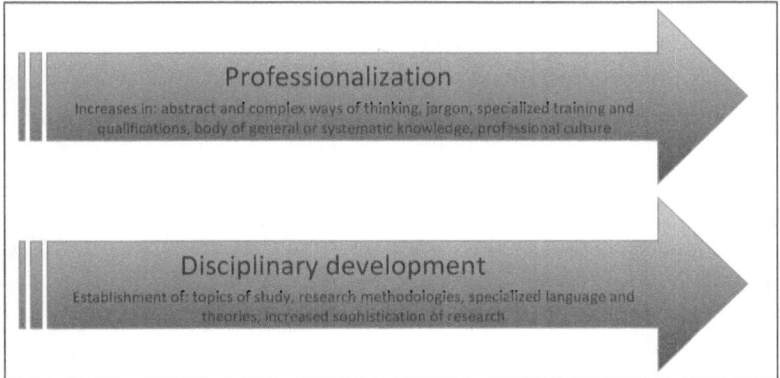

Figure 1. Processes of professionalization and disciplinary development

## Disciplinary and Professional Development of Second Language Writing

To structure my analysis, I have adapted Shneider's four-stage model of disciplinary development to examine where the field of second language writing has been and where it might be at this juncture. The journal, as I note above, is a productive site for such an analysis as it includes numerous components that discursively construct the field. Obviously, published articles are one site of such construction, but I wanted to get beyond that and think of the many other ways in which the field is constructed through journal-related activities, many of which are less public and less visible but still relevant. Toward that goal, I also analyzed a sample of 60 recent manuscript reviews with a range of editorial recommendations, which, together demonstrate values and ideologies and may suggest a presence or absence of an agreed body of knowledge and a characterization of the field and its boundaries. Further, to understand how established L2 writing scholars might feel the journal has changed over its 22-year history, I sent a short survey to 14 professionals with connections to the *JSLW* that date back to its first few years; seven of these experts responded to my survey. The survey asked about respondents' perceptions of any changes over the last 20 years to the field, to the journal's published papers, to how they might author a paper for the *JSLW*, and to their peer reviewing practices for the *JSLW*. In addition, I posted a separate survey on two professional listservs and on Facebook (re-posted by several colleagues), inviting graduate students to participate. Overall, that survey had 45 respondents, with 35 of these meeting my criteria (which were that respondents had to be graduate students who were studying L2 writing as a primary research area and had read at least one article in the *JSLW*). This survey asked respondents for their perceptions about specialist knowledge required for reading the journal and about the journal's accessibility to newcomers in terms of topics, theories, and methodologies. I've attempted to weave these respondents' perspectives into my narrative of the field in the following sections, particularly as I address the current state of the profession as represented in the *JSLW*.

**Stage One: "The Pioneers"**

In Shneider's (2009) four-stage model, "the first evolutionary stage" is a period in which "previously known phenomena become the subject matter of a new scientific field" (p. 217). Because these first-stage scholars are bringing new topics into their analysis, they must also create a new language to describe this subject matter. Shneider's examples from science include differential equations or the model of DNA that later become a shared language within the disciplines. Stage One scholars do not necessarily discover new facts or phenomena, but they create new frameworks for observing and analyzing. These first-stagers tend to be unafraid to make mistakes that will later be corrected as the field develops, and they may focus on multiple interests rather than on a single phenomenon. They might not have exceptional technical skills, Shneider states, but may make use of "philosophical, esthetic and cultural views and/or analogies with funny stories and literature" (p. 219).

In the case of second language writing, Stage One scholarship predates the *JSLW*. As I first read Shneider's description of this first stage, it was hard not to think immediately of Robert B. Kaplan's pioneering work in contrastive rhetoric (Kaplan, 1966). *New framework and language for analysis?* Absolutely—Kaplan's work represents one of the first attempts to analyze L2 writing at a level that went beyond the sentence. *A willingness to make errors that might be amended as the field develops?* Definitely—Kaplan specifically states that much more research is needed to establish what he calls a "meaningful contrastive system" (p. 15). *Expansive scholarly view that brings in multiple disciplines and analogies?* Kaplan's 1966 article draws broadly on work from philosophy, linguistics, rhetoric, and anthropology. Though this work was not the first study of second language writing, it provides an excellent example of the early stage of the field and its development, particularly in the United States.

Pioneering research in second language writing was published in venues like *Language Learning, TESOL Quarterly, ESP Journal, ELT Journal,* and, to a lesser extent, *College Composition and Communication*. These papers reveal the lack of an existing body of field-specific knowledge, as authors were forced to draw on a wide range of other disciplines to inform their work. One of my favorite parts of Kaplan's (1966) paper is footnote 21, in which he very reluctantly cites his own work:

> At the risk of being accused of immodesty, I would recommend in particular the section entitled "outlining" in Robert B. Kaplan, *Reading and Rhetoric* (New York, 1963), pp. 69–80. (Kaplan, 1966, p. 19)

## Stage Two: "The Developers"

In Shneider's (2009) model, Stage Two of disciplinary evolution is characterized by the development of the major tools and approaches for studying a broader range of phenomena. Second-stage science might include breakthroughs that come from applying a methodology from another academic area as a way to re-think or understand a problem. Shneider argues that it is these advancements that are the most cited later on. Second-stage scholars are characterized by "ingenuity and inventiveness, an ability to implement ideas and a high-risk tolerance in the selection of their tasks" (p. 220).

Tony Silva's (1993) article "Toward an Understanding of the Distinct Nature of Second Language Writing" provides one example of this kind of second-stage work. Silva closely analyzed 72 empirical research reports that compared L1 and L2 writing, identifying trends across studies to help create a picture of the various ways in which L2 writing could be seen as distinct from L1 writing. Many of the studies he looked at came from dissertations but also included book chapters and articles from venues like *ELT Journal, Journal of Basic Writing, Language Learning, TESOL Quarterly, World Englishes,* and several regional journals. It was an ambitious attempt to begin to create a body of research and a scholarly conversation. According to Google Scholar, this 1993 article has been cited over 700 times.

Also in the early 1990s, we start to see numerous studies of international student writers in the United States, published by scholars like Ilona Leki and those in Barbara Kroll's important edited collection, *Second Language Writing*. These are names that all will find familiar: Joan Carson, Ulla Connor, Alister Cumming, Liz Hamp-Lyons, Ann Johns, and Joy Reid, to name a few. Works like these helped to establish methodologies for studying L2 writing that are still used today, such as interviews, surveys, and analysis of student texts.

It is within this stage of our story that the *Journal of Second Language Writing* enters the picture. In his 2012 piece in the *JSLW*, titled "*JSLW@20: The Prequel and the Inside Story* (with Several Previously Unpublished Bonus Texts)," Silva (2012) shares the backstory. In short, Tony Silva, a PhD student, met Iona Leki, an associate professor, after one of her talks at the 1989 TESOL convention. As they talked, they lamented the difficulty of being published in second language writing. As Silva writes, "L2 journals were not so interested in writing, and writing journals were not so interested in L2 writing" (2012, p. 187). Some time later, Leki rung up Silva and asked if he would be interested in working with her to establish a new journal; Silva was on board immediately, and the rest, as they say, is history.

The first issue of the *JSLW* was published in January 1992 by Ablex Publishing Corporation, a small company in the northeastern United States. In 1997, after the death of Ablex's founder, Ablex was subsumed under JAI Press. Then, just one year later, Ablex and JAI were bought by the global publishing company Elsevier Science Limited (which is now known as Elsevier). In 2001, the *JSLW* began publishing four—rather than three—issues per year and became available online. With increased recognition, subscriptions, and submission numbers, the journal was, in Silva's words, "on its way to becoming a respected international publication" (p. 3).

Articles published in the early 1990s reflect in many ways the still nascent professionalization of the field. The lead article in the first issue, for example, offers an explicit reflection on the state of the field at the time:

> Although the writing component of ESL has been around as long as the field of ESL itself, its emergence as an independent area of specialization in applied linguistics, with the theoretical development and empirical research of a specialization, has come about only within the last decade. (Santos, 1992, p. 1)

In these earliest *JSLW* articles, the area of scholarship is typically referred to as "ESL writing," and issues are often discussed with reference to L1 writing scholarship. Citations to U S composition studies journals are fairly typical, but also common are references to writing as a component "skill" of language learning, as we see in Santos's (1992) introduction. Most articles in these early years were written by U.S.-based scholars, perhaps influenced by the journal's establishment within the United States, but there are also works by scholars in countries such as Canada, Japan, and Hong Kong. Figure 2 lists the scholars published in the first six issues of the journal—names that will be very recognizable to today's second language professionals.

---

**Volume 1, Issue 1**
- Terry Santos
- **Alister Cumming**
- Joan G. Carson
- Karen E. Johnson

**Volume 1, Issue 2**
- Joy Reid
- Michael Janopoulos
- **Hugh Gosden**
- JoAnne D. Liebman

**Volume 1, Issue 3**
- Gayle L. Nelson, John M. Murphy
- Donna M. Johnson
- **Jane Stanley**
- Kate Mangelsdorf, Ann Schlumberger
- John Hedgcock, Natalie Lefkowitz

Volume 2, Issue 1
- Carol O. Sweedler-Brown
- **Mark N. Brock**
- **Martha C. Pennington, Sufumi So**
- Sandra Lee McKay
- Ann M. Johns
- Terry Santos

Volume 2, Issue 2
- **Pat Currie**
- Dana Ferris
- **Glenn D. Deckert**
- Elaine Tarone, Bruce Downing, Andrew Cohen, Susan Gilette, Robin Murie, Beverly Dailey

Volume 2, Issue 3
- Carol Severino
- JoAnne Devine, Kevin Railey, Philip Boshoff
- **Martha C. Pennington**
- Marianne Phinney, Sandra Khouri

---

Figure 2. Authors in the first six issues of JSLW. Authors based outside of the United States appear in boldface.

Early papers in the *JSLW* are not characterized by heavy jargon. Terminology is typically defined and relates to conceptual and theoretical work in L1 composition studies and/or TESOL and English for Academic Purposes (EAP). Quantitative studies often use descriptive, rather than inferential, statistics and are likely to be accessible to readers who lack graduate coursework in quantitative research.

As a newer field, these early papers describe relatively large research gaps and contributions that are primarily pedagogical, reflecting a practical orientation within a fairly new field of study. We find explicit statements in these early articles that draw our attention to these facts:

> The following is written to add to the current conversations. Because our conversations about academic literacy are so new, I begin with basic notions that provide us a foundation for building new approaches to preparing L2 students for the academic mainstream. (Blanton, 1994, p. 2)

These earliest years of the journal, then, begin to construct a field and an accompanying professional identity. Explicit attention is given to establishing and identifying a distinct body of scholarship, but one that is still new and is strongly linked to second language studies/TESOL or to L1 composition, or in some cases, to both. We also find expansive room for new research, the presence of novel methodological and theoretical approaches, and a general sense of *need* and *excitement* for studying "ESL writing."

This burst of new scholarship that begins to identify itself as part of a field—rather than as a component of another field—is increasingly visible in the *JSLW* by the end of the 1990s. Authors that we now strongly associate with second language writing are prominent in the journal and the journal's reference list, such as: Dwight Atkinson, Christine Pearson Casanave, Dana Ferris, Ken Hyland, Icy Lee, Rosa Manchón, Paul Kei Matsuda, and Neomy Storch. The journal, by this point, has begun to establish new topics of inquiry, and we see continued expansion of authors' geographic locations.

## Stage Three: "The Producers"

The line between Stage Two and Stage Three in disciplinary development is not a clear one. It is likely, for example, that some Stage Two scholarship is published simultaneously with Stage Three scholarship. Gradually, though, we do see a shift over time. In Shneider's (2009) model, Stage Three scholarship includes "the application of known research methods to new research subject matters" (p. 200). It is at this stage that most of the data and knowledge of the discipline is created—and this is good news for today's second language writing scholars, because we are arguably now in this third stage.

Third-stage scholars begin to combine research methods and topics and, as a result, discover new subjects and phenomena. Stage Three research is described by Shneider (2009) as highly professionalized in the sense that both the subject matter and the methods for studying it have now become increasingly sophisticated, drawing on years of knowledge construction by specialists. While Stage One scholars may have broad knowledge in philosophy and art, and may be allowed imprecision and even errors, Stage Three scholars are more specialized and are held to high standards of research. Shneider argues that "the leaders in the field tend to be the neatest, most hard working and detail oriented" (p. 220). The third stage can actually open doors to a new first stage, or the development of a new scientific field. While third-stagers are likely to be open to new methods and technologies, Shneider describes them as "hesitant to welcome first-stage propositions" (p. 220).

Somewhere between the mid-1990s and the early 2000's, most *JSLW* articles begin to reflect these characteristics of a more specialized and professionalized field. There is a growing sense of an existing body of knowledge and a group of people working to contribute to it. That group of people is international, with backgrounds in applied linguistics, TESOL, education, composition studies, and in some cases, all of these areas. By this stage, the field is generally referred to not as "ESL writing" but rather as "second language writing"—an arguably broader and more inclusive term (which also, un-coincidentally, matches the title of the *Journal*).

While early *JSLW* articles made frequent reference to journals like *TESOL Quarterly* and *CCC*, more recent articles heavily reference—unsurprisingly!—the *Journal of Second Language Writing*, as well as a wide range of journals in English for Academic Purposes (EAP), second language studies, and writing studies. This change in referencing patterns reflects both the internationalization of the journal and the existence of a growing body of research on second language writing. Researchers now have closely related prior research to draw upon and theoretical frameworks that have been developed with second language writing and writers in mind.

The areas of research published in the *JSLW* seem to have diversified by Stage Three as well, a point also noted by nearly all of the expert L2 writing scholars who responded to my survey. In comparison with the earliest volumes of the journal, current scholarship includes a wider range of topics, bringing in more work linked to areas like ESP/EAP or SLA, and examining contexts in a fairly wide variety of geographical and educational sites. There also is a growing number of articles on writing in non-English languages, though English definitely still dominates. Figure 3 displays a sample of some of the topics, languages, and contexts addressed in the four issues published in 2014.

- SFL genre-based teaching in K-6 (English, US)
- Textography of international graduate student (English, US)
- Thinking aloud, L2 writing processes, and L2 written text (English, China)
- Teacher assessment of L2 writing (English, Canada)
- Institutional support structures for first-year refugee college students (English, US)
- Mediational means in collaborative business classroom writing (English, Canada)
- Racial and language ideology (English, US)
- Interactional resources in 11-year old L2 letter writing (English, Sweden)
- Motivation and perceptions of feedback practices (German, US)

Figure 3. Sample topics, languages, and contexts represented in JSLW's four issues of 2014.

Jargon has also become more prevalent in the last decade or so of the journal, though it is generally still not impenetrable—perhaps partially due to pressure from review process to make the papers accessible and interesting to the diverse readership. Articles published in 2014 use relatively accessible terms like *textual borrowing, genre, situated social practice, intercultural rhetoric, metacognitive processes, task representations,* and *complexity-accuracy-fluency (CAF)*. Theoretical terms and constructs do appear with some frequency but explanations are typically included within the articles. More opaque jargon tends to be found in quantitative studies that rely on inferential statistics and using terms like *Wilcoxon signed rank test, weighted clause ratio,* and *multiple regression analysis.*

In my survey of graduate students specializing in L2 writing, 82% described the journal as "fairly" or "very" accessible. The 35 respondents described the most accessible topics as written corrective feedback, peer review, collaborative writing, and anything related to teaching and classroom practices. Qualitative research was also mentioned as a methodology that tended to be approachable to newcomers. In contrast, these respondents noted that less accessible topics included: voice, identity, socially oriented research, SLA-SLW interfaces, psycholinguistics, linguistically oriented research, genre, historical research, and research that is tied to contexts with which some readers are unfamiliar. Respondents explained that many of these areas require specialist knowledge, suggesting that the journal now reflects a certain degree of disciplinary professionalization that may make the articles challenging at times for newcomers but still generally readable with some related expertise. One respondent wrote that when he or she first began reading the journal it was:

> . . . not very accessible. It wasn't until my third year [of graduate study] that I felt better able to understand—only after I had classes in language acquisition.

In addition to some increased jargon and a wider range of topics, we see changes in the pressures of communicating novelty and contribution. Today, *JSLW* papers are expected to construct a recognizable body of knowledge and to contribute to it. Authors, in turn, are under increased pressure to demonstrate not just a research gap but also a gap that is important to address. It is not unusual to see peer reviewers note in their comments to authors that "just because a gap exists does not mean it is worth studying." Indeed, in the recent sample of peer reviews I examined, the two most common reasons for rejecting a paper were irreparable flaws in research design and lack of strong contribution to the field. Comments are typically something like, *While this study is well designed and the paper is well written, it unfortunately does not offer anything substantially new to the field*, or, *I'd like to give this author a chance, but I don't think there is enough here to warrant publication in the* JSLW. *Perhaps it can find a home in another journal.*

Authors therefore must locate important problems worthy of addressing and must demonstrate the contributions of their findings. Two experts surveyed pointed to the increased attention that they now give, as reviewers, to a manuscript's contribution. One wrote:

> I've become pickier about whether or not I think a particular piece will be interesting for our readership. If a piece is well executed but on an overdone topic and not written in an engaging way, I'm less inclined to accept it. In other words, just "solid research design" isn't enough (though it's a good start)—it needs to make a useful argument, too. Also, I want the articles to be primarily about writing and not something mainly about technical, narrow SLA issues. There are other journals for that.

Interestingly, today's JSLW articles often frame their contributions in terms of scholarly conversations rather than contributions to classroom practice, as commonly seen in Stage Two scholarship. We frequently find authors describing how their research *challenges, extends,* or *complicates* existing knowledge, all metaphors that rely on the assumption of an existing body of work. What that body of work encompasses—and what is does not—is of course not clear-cut. It is these comments about contributions to "the field" that are perhaps most interesting and instructive.

In the 2013 Disciplinary Dialogue section of the *JSLW*, 11 scholars in the field responded to the question posed by editor Dwight Atkinson: "What is second language writing?" Similarly, manuscript reviews and editorial decisions that identify a paper's contribution to "the field" clearly invoke some sense of an existing field, and they imply boundaries, but the constructions of those boundaries are not always shared. What may be "in the field" to one expert may be "better suited to another journal" to another.

One additional pressure here is the increased competition for publication space in the journal. The *JSLW* received 40 to 50 manuscripts per year in the early 1990s and had an acceptance rate around 20%; in 2014, the number of submissions was just over 250, pushing the acceptance rate down to around 7%, and submissions continue to rise. Several of the long-time experts in my survey made note of this increased competition in the review process. As one wrote:

> The journal has become more rigorous, demanding, and competitive for publication as the field has grown internationally and as the professional definition of L2 writing has moved beyond ESL in North American universities to include schools,

other languages taught or learned, and other educational contexts and populations.

Two experts in my survey also described themselves as having become more rigorous reviewers over time. One saw this change "largely as a reflection of the field's (and my own) evolving knowledge base and my rising expectations for rigor, quality, and clarity." At the same time, this scholar wrote, "Regrettably, I am more likely now to recommend outright rejections than I was in the past."

Other scholars' comments caution us about some negative side-effects of increased rigor and competition. For example, one expert in my survey wrote:

> I worry that the standards of rigor might have gone too far in the direction of the elevation of sophisticated statistical techniques.... I worry that we are not paying enough attention to the design of meaningful research and not committing ourselves to the more lengthy and complex topics that might help us understand L2 writers and writing better.

Perceptions of increased competition may also threaten the very positive sense of the community that has tended to characterize our field. One expert wrote:

> I've found it tougher as an author to get things through the reviewers than I did back in the 90s.... I've also had a couple of my students treated pretty roughly (and in my opinion, unfairly) by the *JSLW* review process. Rigor is good, but there's no such thing as a perfect piece, either.

And:

> ... I have heard from more than a handful of colleagues who have submitted [manuscripts] in the past several years that they have found some peer evaluations and editorial recommendations to be on the harsh (indeed, nit-picky) side.... Some friends of [the] *JSLW* perceive the journal's selectivity to have become potentially excessive (suggesting that it may have lost some of the spirit of collegial support for which it was formerly known).

At the same time, another scholar wrote:

> I have an impression that reviewers of [the] *JSLW* tend to be kinder and more constructive, and less harsh than reviewers of other journals, and that has not changed. It reflects the warm and welcoming atmosphere of the field itself, which I hope will not change in the future, too.

## WHAT LIES AHEAD?

Although Shneider's (2009) model of disciplinary development includes four stages, my narrative of the *JSLW* and L2 writing remains in Stage Three. In the fourth stage of Shneider's model, prior disciplinary knowledge is applied to practical activities, keeping the knowledge alive and relevant. Examples include fields like physics or classical philology. This is where the model breaks down a bit for our field, for which the application of disciplinary knowledge to practice has always been at the heart of what we do. However Stage Four manifests itself, though, it is likely a ways off for second language writing. For now, we are, arguably, at an extremely interesting time in our field's history and professional trajectory. But I want to end my discussion by considering two issues of caution as we imagine the journal's and the field's futures.

The first of the two tensions that linger in my mind relates to a quote that I shared earlier in this chapter: "Every constituted profession must continue to defend its rights and its borders" (Ohmann, 1990, p. 250). On the one hand, the growing diversity of scholarship within the *JSLW* is a welcome and celebrated development in both the journal and the field. At the same time, as the research net widens, we will, I suspect, increasingly wrestle with the issue of what constitutes "the field." Peer reviews and editorial discussions suggest an increased awareness of an existing field that should be preserved—or even protected—from other encroaching areas of research. The relationship between second language writing and SLA, for example, is constantly being constructed through manuscripts, manuscript reviews, and even less formal communications among editors and board members. The recent growth of interest in translingualism in U.S. composition studies is another area that often prompts lively discussions about scholarly territory (see, for example, Atkinson *et al.*, 2015).

While such border-struggles are part of any profession, they do raise questions for a flagship journal that has historically played some role in defining the profession. In the 2013 Disciplinary Dialogue discussion referred to earlier, Paul Kei Matsuda highlights the participants' "refusal to draw a clear boundary that delimits the field" (Matsuda, 2013, p. 449). He also recognizes the continued expansion of the field's scope, and notes that it has been aided by the new directions that are intentionally sought through *JSLW* special issues or themes addressed at the Symposium on Second Language Writing. But to what extent can the *JSLW* sustain this widening of topics and research methodologies within a fairly specialized area while retaining a dedicated readership? As even more specialized journals enter the scene (such as the new *Journal of Response to Writing*), will the *JSLW* become somewhat analogous to *TESOL Quarterly*, with a little for everyone but perhaps not a lot for anyone? Or will such breadth in scope even matter in an age in which print copies of journals are increasingly rare, and very few readers have the time or inclination to read a journal from front to back? As the field and the *Journal* continue to develop and address a wider range of issues, these are questions that the editors and editorial board members will grapple with.

A second tension relates to the field's proud identity as a welcoming and supportive scholarly community and, simultaneously, a perception among at least some long-time SLW scholars of an increased—and maybe inappropriate—level of rigor in a publishing environment that has become more and more competitive. How can the *JSLW* retain its collegial and supportive community identity with the heavy volume of submissions and the reality that more and more high-quality papers will not find a home in the *Journal*? How can the editors and reviewers continue to ensure that cutting edge and less traditional work can make it through the editorial gates and that the voices of newer and off-networked scholars can still be represented?

Obviously, I have no immediate answers to these questions, but it is also not my place to have answers. As Silva (2012) describes in his reflection of *JSLW@20*:

> *JSLW* has always been a group effort, its success dependent, over the last two decades, on the participation of thousands of readers, hundreds of submitters and authors, dozens of reviewers [now likely in the hundreds] and editorial board members, numerous editorial assistants, four [now five] editors, three publishing houses, and four [now six] universities. (p. 192)

And, so, I pose it to the readers to continue to imagine and construct the profession in the next 20 years.

## NOTE

1. See, for example, the discussion in the 2013 Disciplinary Dialogue addressing "What Is Second Language Writing" in the *Journal of Second Language Writing*.

## REFERENCES

Atkinson, D. (2013). Introduction. *Journal of Second Language Writing, 22*, 425.

Atkinson, D., Crusan, D., Matsuda, P. K., Ortmeier-Hooper, C., Ruecker, T., Simpson, S., & Tardy, C. M. (2015). Clarifying the relationship between L2 writing and translingual writing: An open letter to writing studies editors and organization leaders. *College English, 77*, 383–386.

Blanton, L. L. (1994). Discourse, artifacts, and the Ozarks: Understanding academic literacy. *Journal of Second Language Writing, 3*, 1–17.

Kaplan, R. B. (1966). Cultural thought patterns in inter-cultural education. *Language Learning, 16*(1), 1–20.

Krishnan, A. (2009). What are academic disciplines? Some observations on the disciplinarity vs. interdisciplinarity debate. *ESRC National Centre for Research Methods Working Paper*. Available at: http://eprints.ncrm.ac.uk/783/1/what_are_academic_disciplines.pdf

Matsuda, P. K. (2013). Response: What *is* second language writing—and why does it matter? *Journal of Second Language Writing, 22*, 448–450.

Ohmann, R. (1990). Graduate students, professionals, intellectuals. *College English, 52*(3), 247–257.

Ritzer, G. (1975). Professionalization, bureaucratization and rationalization: The views of Max Weber. *Social Forces, 53*(4), 627–634.

Santos, T. (1992). Ideology in composition: L1 and ESL. *Journal of Second Language Writing, 1*, 1–15.

Shneider, A. M. (2009). Four stages of a scientific discipline; four types of scientist. *Trends in Biomedical Sciences, 34*(5), 217–223.

Silva (1993). Toward an understanding of the distinct nature of L2 writing: The ESL research and its implications. *TESOL Quarterly, 27*, 657–677.

Silva, T. (2012). *JSLW@20*: The prequel and the inside story (with several previously unpublished bonus texts). *Journal of Second Language Writing, 21*, 187–194.

Weber, M. (1968). *Economy and society*. Totowa, NJ: Bedminster.

# 2 Where It All Begins: Doctoral Studies as Professional Development in Second Language Writing

*Dwight Atkinson*

Professional scholarly development obviously begins in graduate school—the soil in which we first plant our roots.[1] But what kind of roots are these that grow up *into* the plant as well as down and out? In Geertz's (1983) words, "the various disciplines . . . are . . . ways of being in the world. . . . [To join a discipline is] not just to take up a technical task but to take on a cultural frame which defines a great part of one's life" (p. 155). In other words, becoming a professional scholar means adopting a *form of life* (Wittgenstein, 1953/2001).[2]

In this chapter, I will assume that professional development in graduate school means, quite substantially, taking on at least one form of life. I will have little to say about the "form of life" concept itself, beyond noting here that it has a profound history in educational thought as a direct development of *Bildung*, the concept on which the whole idea of the research university is based (Beiser, 2003; Cahill, 2011; "Wilhelm von Humboldt," 2007/2011; Watson, 2010), and is intimately connected, as Geertz also suggests, to the concept of culture (e.g., Williams, 1983). Instead, I will discuss how we might *nurture* forms of life in SLW, specifically at the doctoral level.

## ONCE UPON A TIME?

Once upon a time, or so the story goes, professors told their doctoral students not to worry and not to hurry: Let it come; don't force it. First, soak up the knowledge, and then (and *only* then) let your research focus and disciplinary identity emerge. From this viewpoint doctoral work is a natural process—like digestion, first language acquisition, or love—so let it develop naturally.

In fact, I don't know if those days ever really existed, but if they did I'm convinced they're gone. Instead, I'd like to argue here that if PhD students want to develop strong professional identities, they need to start from Day 1 (or at least Day 2): attending conferences, networking, researching, collaborating, reading, reading, reading, and writing (and writing and writing), etc. Likewise from Day 1, faculty members need to foster, promote, encourage, support, and exhort.

"But hold on," you say, "People do doctorates for all kinds of reasons: Being a scholar and researcher is just one of them. Some plan to be teachers or administrators; some may even want to be poets or photographers; others don't need jobs at all. And how about those students who just don't know—who are testing the waters or finding their feet? Did you, Dwight Atkinson, know what you were doing from the moment you entered your doctoral program?"

Here's my response, at least to the first question (I'll save my answer to the second for the conclusion of this chapter): Students in flight school are trained seriously to be pilots; law students undergo arduous training to be lawyers; medical students do years of challenging schooling, followed by years of stressful apprenticeship, followed by years of even more stressful residency to become doctors; engineering and science students complete difficult coursework at both the undergraduate and graduate levels, and do rigorous apprenticeships in labs. Why should SLW be different? If students from any of the above-mentioned fields happen to learn in their programs something other than the tools of the trade and the spirit by which those tools are animated, that's wonderful—more power to them. But in what sense are they professionally qualified if they don't know the basic tools of their trade and the spirit in which they are meant to be applied?

What doctoral work in SLW should offer, I believe, is intensive training in the field's signature tools, which are first and foremost the tools of research and scholarship. Certainly, we can learn all kinds of things in graduate school, including how to be better teachers or administrators. But spending 5-plus years completing coursework, taking exams, and writing a dissertation is not the best way to become a better teacher; there are much more efficient and effective ways. Conversely, being better teachers or administrators isn't particular to the doctoral form of life. Our main job as faculty can therefore only be to guide our students in acquiring our professional tribe's professional qualifications—our special capital and special power. Research and scholarship are what set us apart, and these are what our students need to be trained in.

The best way to do this, I submit, is to invite our students into—no, to invite our students to *dive into*—this form of life. "How?" you ask? Here are eight ways among many:

1. By providing good, active role models from Day 1;
2. By assigning not just response papers and/or annotated bibliographies but also full-blown term papers;
3. By giving meaningful comments on those term papers—comments that help students learn the literate tools of the trade;
4. By encouraging students to submit those papers to conferences;
5. By encouraging students to attend those conferences even if they *don't* get accepted;
6. By encouraging students to do collaborative research;
7. By promoting and facilitating networking; and
8. By giving students *the time* to do these things—not by turning them into teaching machines.

Equally and essentially, students must take every opportunity to dive in.

## Tools of the Trade

So far I have stated a general message: For the sake of their professional development, doctoral students need to be actively inducted into and trained—and to creatively and agentively engage—in the form of life known as SLW. Let me now get more specific.

### Networking

Let me begin, in fact, with an activity which by no means represents a signature activity of our field, but which is nonetheless vitally important: *networking*. My justification for doing so has two parts: 1) Like other disciplines, SLW is essentially a community endeavor, so becoming part of the SLW community is critical to taking on its form(s) of life; and 2) the Symposium on Second Language Writing (SSLW)—the conference for which this paper was originally written, and which thus inevitably influences its rhetorical purpose—is without question the best networking site for SLW in the world.

First, then, why is networking so important? The answer of course is that face-to-face interaction—the "primordial site of [human] sociality" (Schegloff, 2006, p. 70)—is the most fundamental means of establishing socio-professional relationships too. Without networking, one is just another face in the crowd—or not even a face if one doesn't attend conferences, which are our main community-building endeavors. If, for example, a graduate student council is being formed at a professional organization (as happened recently at the American Association for Applied Linguistics), or a "junior editorial board" is being set up at an academic journal (as happened recently at *English for Specific Purposes*), who will be invited to participate? Someone the organizers don't know? Or someone equally qualified who they've met at conferences and had interesting conversations with? The answer is obvious: I can honestly say that almost nothing good that's happened to me in SLW or applied linguistics happened because I *didn't* know someone—because I *didn't* have a network.

One wonderful thing about the SLW field is that it is relatively flat—there are no real rock stars or prima donnas like there are in some other fields. If, as a student, you attend the receptions at SSLW, for instance, you're likely to find Tony Silva or Chris Tardy or Paul Kei Matsuda or Icy Lee just standing there chatting. And if you wait for a while and then address them appropriately—or if that's too challenging (and sometimes it is), then you ask your professor to introduce you to them—they'll be happy to talk to you too.

But here's some frank advice: Don't waste the opportunity. Don't, for instance, ask to pose for a picture with the scholar and then run off and put it on Facebook. Don't do this, at least, if you want them to remember you. To leave an impression, have an academic conversation: Ask an academic question; offer an academic comment; talk about something they've written; talk about something *you've* written. Build your academic identity by playing the academic game.[3]

The academic game is not about collecting pictures: That's a *different* game. Instead, put yourself in the academic scene and connect with others academically, so that you (1) build your professional identity and (2) build the field. The two are closely connected: Students won't develop professionally if they don't develop socially, i.e., if they don't actively join the community. And a field can't build or even maintain itself without new ideas and new conversations; that is, without inducting new scholar-members. Without new members, communities rapidly disappear (Wenger, 1998). Networking is a highly efficient way to do these two things together: to locate yourself squarely in the field, and to begin to make your contribution to it.

To summarize my main points in this section: Networking is vitally important for establishing a scholarly identity and building a field. And SLW scholars are more likely to remember you if you give them something academic to chew on: A question, a comment, or an idea.

**Academic Writing**

I turn now to what surely *is* a signature activity of our SLW tribe: academic writing. Let me begin very generally.

In his popular book *Outliers* (2008), Malcolm Gladwell argued that certain complex and socially valued human skills take thousands of hours to become expert in. Gladwell's examples involve sports, music, and computer programming, but they could easily be extended to the visual and performing arts, professional-level engine repair, professional cooking, high-level computer gaming, flying, technical climbing, and advanced second language learning. Academic writing as well is a prime candidate for Gladwell's list.

Based on a series of cases and statistical calculations, Gladwell suggested that there is something like a magic minimal amount of time one needs in order to develop expertise in these complex activities: 10,000 hours. He argued that the most successful professional people—including geniuses like Mozart and Bill Gates—spent enormous amounts of time day after day over many years becoming experts. Gladwell of course wasn't arguing that, by spending all those hours, you or I will become a Bill Gates or Mozart; his point was rather that without being deeply immersed in developing expertise in certain complex activities over many years, one will never become expert in those activities.

Let's now do some simple math based on Gladwell's magic number: 10,000 hours. 10,000 hours is 2.75 hours a day, 365 days a year, over a period of 10 years—*almost 12% of a 24-hour day, or approximately 16% if we factor in 8 hours a day for sleeping!* If we reduce the training period to 5 years, that's 5.5 hours a day, 365 days a year—*24% of a 24-hour day, or 33% if 8 hours are subtracted for sleeping!* Now this is impossible, isn't it? Does anyone really devote one-third of their waking life every day for 5 years to academic writing, or research, or maybe even their whole professional life?

Gladwell's numbers certainly look a bit extreme to me (although high-level musicians, athletes, medical doctors, and engineers in the making must often spend this many hours over many years perfecting their skills). But I take his general point quite seriously: If you want to become an expert and/or professional, you need to work long and hard. You need to devote a great part of your life to doing your field's signature activities so much that they become automatic and a part of you—not things that each time you do them you say, "I hate this," or "I'll do it tomorrow," or "Yuck, this is not for me."

To summarize my main argument so far in this section: If you don't start to see yourself as a budding academic writer or expert in the making—if you don't see yourself as doing the things academic writers conventionally do or as inhabiting the kinds of identities they conventionally inhabit, and particularly if you don't write intensively in an academic mode over a multi-year period—then, quite simply, you won't become an academic writer, and you won't become an established member of your academic/professional field. More generally, if you don't perform the complex activities associated with scholarly expertise in SLW habitually and devotedly, or develop the form(s) of life in which and for which such activities are conventionally done, you are unlikely to become an SLW professional—at least an academic/scholarly one.

Turning now to academic writing as a specific phenomenon: First, it's too late to learn to write academically *after* graduating—that's like primary school students learning to read *after* primary school. Both are core academic tools, though at very different levels, so they must be learned sooner rather than later. Likewise, faculty members need to play their part by actively apprenticing doctoral students into the mysteries of academic writing, as perhaps the most significant part of their graduate training. Doing so is not easy and takes an enormous amount of time; and since different students have different learning approaches (biosocial diversity being a defining trait of human beings—Evans & Levinson, 2009) such "cognitive apprenticeships" (see Atkinson, 1997) need to be custom-designed (Belcher, 1994; Cho, 2004; Simpson & Matsuda, 2008). But professors who don't take their formative role in such expert-apprentice relationships seriously are simply abdicating their duty.

Second, let's try to analyze this thing called academic writing a little more closely. It is not just one thing—that's for certain (e.g., MacDonald, 2010)—but let's assume for a moment that it is. Academic writing—at least in the North American academy and at least in one of its archetypal forms, the research article—may *look* like other kinds of writing because it uses many of the same symbol systems, the vocabularies overlap, and it has many of the same textual conventions. But based on these similarities can it be concluded that the main purpose of academic writing is simply to communicate meaning—simply to get our message across, as with some other kinds of writing?

In my opinion, academic writing isn't just another form of communication. Instead, it is a *knowledge-injection system:* a highly efficient mechanism for injecting highly specific forms of knowledge into a knowledge-based capitalist/competitive economy (Atkinson, 2003). That is, academic writing is a technology for making messages that can efficiently be turned into forms of capital (Bourdieu, 1986). This explains why the tools in our toolkit are so highly developed and so precisely aimed at efficient consumption: titles; abstracts; keywords; purpose statements; research questions; highly standardized sectioning conventions like Introduction-Methods-Results-Discussion; standard rhetorical move sequences within sections (e.g., Swales, 1990); logically developed paragraphs, often with explicit topic sentences; advance organizers; and discourse markers like "In this paper," "Therefore," "For example," or "In sum." Professional academic writing is all these things, *plus* an almost endless process of revising, until the information is melted down into maximally consumable form.

None of the features just mentioned are designed to express highly personal meaning in a free or genre-bending form. Quite the opposite: As I've already suggested, academic writing is a highly specific and highly developed technology for injecting a limited set of meanings into a knowledge system—more like a computer program or mathematical symbol system, in this sense, than abstract painting or do-it-yourself home repair. So if academic writing really *is* a high-level literate technology with highly specific tools, then it really *is* a different animal than what we generally call writing. It *looks* similar, but it is not the same thing. This has real consequences, including for learning.

It is sometimes said that learning to write academically—learning to operate this complex literate technology—is a kind of second language learning. I don't know to what extent this is true, but my 20 years of experience working with graduate students on their theses and dissertations tells me two things: 1) that most students, no matter how categorized—"multilingual" or "native" or "generation 1.5," etc.—find this technology alien and not that easy to learn; and 2) that virtually anyone *can* learn this technology if they devote themselves to it and take it seriously—if they throw themselves into it and give it time. The job of faculty is to promote this process in all ways possible, and the job of PhD students is to throw themselves into it.

## Research

Before concluding, let me briefly consider the other signature activity our scholarly profession requires, as mentioned earlier: Research. By research, I mean of course the concepts, tools, techniques, and practices we employ to learn something about the world—more or less systematically—that separate us from laypeople trying to do something similar. What are PhD programs for, if not for learning such tools? Here is one well-known research methodologist's view:

> Skilled research is a craft, and like any craft, it is learned by apprenticeship to competent researchers, by hands-on experience, and by continual practice. It seems remarkable, if we stop to think about it, that research competence is assumed to be gained by learning abstract rules of scientific procedure. Why should such "working knowledge" be learned any more easily, or through other ways, than the competence required for playing the violin or blowing glass or throwing pots? (Mishler, 1990, p. 422)

If Mishler is right—and I have every reason to think he is—then we professors need to teach how to *do* things when we teach research methods, not just *about* them. It's like teaching violin, or glass blowing, or pottery, as Mishler tells us. Likewise, we need to give students plentiful opportunities for practice *beyond* their research methods classes by providing opportunities to learn by doing—doing pre-studies and pilot studies and case studies and *then* dissertation studies. As a first real research experience, dissertation research is too late; the process has to start from the beginning.

## CONCLUSION

Let me conclude in two steps: first, by answering a question and, second, by doing what all practicing academics should do habitually if they care about making new knowledge—quibbling.[4] First, then, let me answer a question introduced at the beginning of this chapter, which went more or less like this: "You say, Dwight Atkinson, that PhD students need to be fully committed and on task—researching, writing, going to conferences, and networking—basically doing everything that more experienced SLW scholars do, from Day 1. You say it's too late for students to figure this out as they go along, or after they're finished. But what about *you*, Dwight Atkinson? Did *you* have it all figured out from Day 1?"

The answer, of course, is no. I entered my PhD program intending to be a university teacher in Japan, where I'd been teaching the previous six years. I thought a doctorate would give me a professional advantage. But from Day 1 I saw what others were doing around me and what my professors were preparing me to do—researching, networking, collaborating, presenting, writing (and writing and writing)—and I followed suit. This was not because I was talented or particularly smart or even particularly academic; rather, it was because I was thrown into a world where research and scholarship mattered: a scholarly form of life. And by doing these things, by practicing them intensively—by *living* them—I became a scholar.

And now for my quibble: The terms "professional development" and "professionalizing," as used so prominently in the SLW field and elsewhere, capture something important: I have used them myself in this chapter's title and throughout. But they also feel a bit distant and perhaps inaccurate—they may even be what Matsuda (2003) called "misnomers." Could this be because they are nominalizations (or at least nominalization-based: "professionalizing" is a nominalization-based gerund)—dynamic processes frozen by language into things, elements, or items (Halliday, 1988)? Somehow, this makes the activities they describe sound like options—items on a menu, selections—something one can take a workshop on, get a certificate in, or have a conference about. But I don't think professional development is optional—far from it. I think it's the *very essence of what we do in our professional scholarly form of life.* Networking, scholarship, research, collaboration, writing (and writing and writing): For me, at least, *these* are what SLW is made of.

## Notes

1. I am well aware that not all SLW professionals define themselves as "scholars." As signaled in the title of this paper and throughout, my main audience is PhD students and faculty—i.e., those who are studying to be or already are scholars.

2. "Form of life" is the concept Wittgenstein (1953/2001) introduced to account for how individuals make sense of language in its everyday uses, which are characteristically indeterminate/merely indexical vis-à-vis much more complex realities. That is, they are only very partial representations of what they are intended to express. Wittgenstein suggested that it was only by being a member of a language-using community/form of life that we make sense of language as used within that form of life. I use the term somewhat more broadly in this paper, as it has often been used since Wittgenstein and his fellow analytic philosophers coined it, to mean something akin to a community of practice (Wenger, 1998) or disciplinary "thought style" (Fleck, 1981).

3. Following the talk on which this chapter is based, a student told me that taking selfies with established SLW scholars was actually a clever strategy for getting to know these scholars professionally. That is, by taking a picture with an established SLW scholar, you now had something to send them by email, and thus had an additional opportunity to establish an academic connection with them.

4. Or as my dissertation advisor Robert B. Kaplan put it so vividly in a recent email, "Faculty are the guardians of discomfort."

## References

Atkinson, D. (1997). A critical approach to critical thinking in TESOL. *TESOL Quarterly, 31,* 71–94.

Atkinson, D. (2003). Writing and culture in the post-process era. *Journal of Second Language Writing, 12,* 49–63.

Beiser, F. (2003). The concept of *Bildung* in early German romanticism. Chapter 4 of *The romantic imperative* (pp. 88–105). Cambridge, MA: Harvard University Press.

Belcher, D. (1994). The apprenticeship approach to advanced academic literacy: Graduate students and their mentors. *English for Specific Purposes, 13,* 23–34.

Bourdieu, P. (1986). The forms of capital. In J. G. Richardson (Ed.), *Handbook of theory and research for the sociology of education* (pp. 241–258). New York: Greenwood Press.

Cahill, K. (2011). *The fate of wonder: Wittgenstein's critique of metaphysics and modernity.* New York: Columbia University Press.

Cho, S. (2004). Challenges of entering discourse communities through publishing in English: Perspectives of nonnative-speaking doctoral students in the United States of America. *Journal of Language, Identity, and Education, 3,* 47–72.

Evans, N., & Levinson, S. (2009). The myth of language universals: Language diversity and its importance for cognitive science. *Behavioral and Brain Sciences, 32,* 429–492.

Fleck, L. (1981). *Genesis and development of a scientific fact.* Chicago: University of Chicago Press.

Geertz, C. (1983). *Local knowledge: Further essays in interpretive anthropology.* New York: Basic Books.

Gladwell, M. (2008). *Outliers: The story of success.* New York: Little, Brown, & Company.

Halliday, M. (1988). On the language of physical science. In M. Ghaddessy (Ed.), *Registers of written English* (pp. 162–178). London: Pinter Publishers.

Matsuda, P. K. (2003). Process and post-process: A discursive history. *Journal of Second Language Writing, 12,* 65–83.

Mishler, E. (1990). Validation in inquiry-guided research: The role of exemplars in narrative studies. *Harvard Educational Review, 60,* 415–442.

Peck-MacDonald, S. (2010). *Professional academic writing in the humanities and social sciences.* Carbondale, IL: Southern Illinois University Press.

Schegloff, E. (2006). Interaction: The infrastructure for social institutions, the natural ecological niche for language, and the arena in which culture is enacted. In N. Enfield & S. Levinson (Eds.), *Roots of human sociality* (pp. 70–96). Oxford: Berg.

Simpson, S., & Matsuda, P. K. (2008). Mentoring as a long-term relationship: Situated learning in a doctoral program. In C. P. Casanave & X. Li (Eds.), *Learning the literacy practices of graduate school: Insiders' reflections on academic enculturation* (pp. 90–104). Ann Arbor: University of Michigan Press.

Wilhelm von Humboldt. (2007/2011). In *Stanford encyclopedia of philosophy.* Retrieved from http://plato.stanford.edu/entries/wilhelm-humboldt/

#RetGerPubEduPol

Swales, J. (1990). *Genre analysis: English in academic and research settings.* Cambridge: Cambridge University Press.

Watson, P. (2010). *The German genius: Europe's third renaissance, the second scientific revolution, and the twentieth century.* New York: Harper Perennial.

Wenger, E. (1998). *Communities of practice.* Cambridge: Cambridge University Press.

Williams, R. (1983). *Keywords: A vocabulary of culture and society.* London: Oxford University Press.

Wittgenstein, L. (1953/2001). *Philosophical investigations.* London: Blackwell.

# 3 Negotiating an Academic Position as an L2 Writing Specialist: The Case of a Second Language (L2) Writing Specialist in a Joint Appointment

*Pisarn Bee Chamcharatsri*

With the rise of interdisciplinary research in academia, hiring practices need to adjust to serve this new era. Second language (L2) writing is no exception because "language and writing issues are multifaceted" (Matsuda, 2013, p. 448). Joint-appointment hiring is one of many approaches that universities have attempted to promote research across disciplines by asking two departments to craft one job description. There are many challenges that faculty in joint-appointment positions have to negotiate. I faced a few dilemmas and challenges when I first started the position. How many meetings should I attend? What would happen to courses that need to be taught if I were to take on a role of an administrator? Should I have one or two office locations? What would happen if I were not happy or welcome in one of the departments? Would I be accepted as a full member of either of the departments? In this chapter, I share my own experience as a joint appointment and how I turn this complex position into an advantage in constructing my scholarly identity. I will conclude with implications for future L2 writing professionals who find themselves in joint-appointment positions in academia.

## A Tale of Two Departments

Many institutions come up with the idea of creating jobs that can serve the needs of two or more programs and/or departments with the hope that these joint positions will promote cross- and inter-disciplinary research and collaboration across programs, departments, and colleges. The issue of balancing the workload of a joint appointment is challenging because colleagues in departments expect the joint appointees to be committed to the same amount of work as those who serve in one department. Smith (2006), who shares the experiences with a joint appointment, pointed out that being in a joint appointment has the perks of working with different faculty, undergraduate, and graduate students; providing interdisciplinary perspectives in faculty meetings; and opening up more opportunities in grant writing proposals. This arrangement creates an opportunity for the joint appointees in terms of teaching, research, and service. At the same time, it can create some challenges at different levels. One aspect of joint appointments that many publications have touched on is the issue of workload (Smith, 2006; Alsup, 2009; National Academy of Sciences, 2005). Departments are usually expecting faculty to not only teach, conduct research studies and publish in refereed journals; they also expect faculty to do service and advise students. Other challenges are the scheduling conflicts of departmental meetings and the process of tenure and promotion. It is recommended to the joint appointees attend to learn about the departmental climates, share thoughts and comments, and become a full member of the department.

Before I had my campus visit, I prepared myself by visiting and doing some research on the university, colleges and departments. I looked up faculty members, what they teach, and their research interests. I also thought of courses I could create and contribute to the departments. Since this was my first time applying for tenure-track positions in the US, I only thought of what I could contribute to the departments. During the three-day visit, I met with faculty members, students, chairs of two departments, and deans from two colleges. I was approached by two search committee members from each department to consider being housed in their departments. While I was meeting with one of the departmental chairs, I was asked to consider choosing his department as my tenure home. My expectation was I would have time to decide after I was offered the job. That was not the case. When I received the phone call from the head of the search committee, I had to make my decision right away because the offer letter would be written by the department in which I chose to receive tenure. I consulted with David Hanauer, my dissertation chair, about the decision I had to make. He recommended that I choose Education as my tenure home because I would have more opportunities to work with graduate students. After I conveyed my decision to the search chair, he was pleased that I chose the College of Education as my tenure home. The negotiation of workload was important because the teaching load in Education is higher than in other colleges; that is, faculty members are expected to teach three courses in one semester and two in the other. With the arrangement of the joint appointment, the department chair made the offer that I would teach only two courses for each semester because of the expectations for attending meetings in two programs, departments, and colleges. I also asked about the expectation of tenure and promotion. I was informed that the tenure home would be the one which made the decision while the other department could provide letters of support.

After joining the University of New Mexico (UNM) as a tenure-track assistant professor with a joint appointment, I met with one of my colleagues who was another joint appointee in Education and English. She became my informal mentor and helped me navigate the position. I often sought her advice regarding meetings, workload, and departmental cultures. She also recommended that I attend meetings in both departments to gain first hand experiences of departmental cultures. We also discussed the expectations for tenure and promotion as joint appointees.

Because I was new to the institution, I attended faculty orientations on the issue of tenure and promotion from both departments. In the orientations, the discussions focused on three major criteria: teaching, research, and service, but they did not discuss how these criteria are applied to joint-appointment situations, so I approached the department chairs to ask for guidelines. For teaching, I was advised to cross list my courses for undergraduate and graduate students in both departments. For research, the answer was to follow the guidelines of my tenure home. Since my tenure home was in Education, I was expected to follow the handbook policy that asked for faculty in Education to produce a minimum of six peer-reviewed publications. For service, I worked on different committees for both departments. When the annual review of tenure and promotion came around, the chair in Education had the power to make the recommendation for my promotion while the chair and colleagues in the English department could write letters of support during the tenure and promotion process.

Having a joint appointment is playing a crucial role in my identity construction as an emerging L2 writing specialist. I decided to learn about the communities of practice in both Education and English (Lave & Wenger, 1991). I made a decision to attend meetings in both departments to learn about their discourse communities. The discourse community in the Bilingual/TESOL program in Education focused on teacher preparation, bilingual education, and teaching English as a second/foreign language. The Rhetoric and Writing program in English focused on first-year composition, professional writing, and writing across communities. When I attended meetings, I asked questions relating to L2 writing such as the frequency of offering L2 writing courses or concerns in working with L2 writers at the undergraduate and graduate levels. The historical knowledge and questions relating to working with L2 writers helped me construct my identity as a L2 writing specialist and a promise of making L2 writing scholarship visible in both departments.

## From Pennsylvania to New Mexico

Scholarship in the field of L2 writing is interdisciplinary. When I was a graduate student in the Composition & TESOL program at Indiana University of Pennsylvania (IUP), Composition teachers defined themselves as "compositionists," whom Matsuda (2006) described in "The Myth of Linguistic Homogeneity in U.S. College Composition" as not interested in scholarship relating to ESL or L2 writing, or "TESOL," which means they do not assume that L2 writing is part of the field of composition studies. It was frustrating to have my peers put me in a box. After reading Matsuda's (2006) article, I made every effort to bring L2 writing into composition courses I took during my graduate studies. I was recognized as an "ESL" person among my composition peers because I always brought up scholarship in L2 writing among my composition peers in class discussions. Through L2 writing scholarship, I became the liaison person between composition and TESOL. I had not imagined that I would have the chance to utilize knowledge I gained from both Composition and TESOL programs to use every day in my tenure track position as a joint appointment in Bilingual/

TESOL program in the College of Education and in the Rhetoric and Writing program in the College of Arts and Sciences at the University of New Mexico (UNM).

In terms of instruction, my teaching load is divided between both programs and departments. I am responsible for teaching one course for the Bilingual/TESOL program and one course in the Rhetoric and Writing program. Since programs have expressed their interest in the need to expand their programs to include adult ESL learners and L2 writing, I can demonstrate that L2 writing is a "'transdisciplinary field' because the intellectual work in the field transcends various disciplinary and institutional structures" (Matsuda, 2013, p. 448) through course readings. In Bilingual/TESOL, the majority of faculty members are bilingual speakers and have educational backgrounds in first and second language acquisition. They also understand issues in language learning and the writing issues of K-12 bilingual students. I was hired as an addition to the program focusing on the scholarship of adult ESL learners. I was given opportunities to offer new graduate courses on teaching adult learners, and I created two courses: Adult ESL Pedagogy and Identities of Adult ESL Learners. In these two courses, I have a mix of graduate students from Rhetoric and Writing and TESOL programs; I always include readings on the scholarship of L2 writing.

In the Rhetoric and Writing program, building a sustainable L2 writing program is important because the University of New Mexico has attracted many international students. However, the first-year composition (FYC) offering for L2 writers was inconsistent in the past due to the lack of L2 writing specialists. I was hired with the assignment to create presence and awareness of L2 writing in the program and to direct an L2 writing program in the future. I was responsible for creating an FYC course for L2 writers (ENGL110) for fall semester and advanced composition for L2 writers (ENGL120) for spring semester. I approached the administrative staff who helped with scheduling of classes. The staff made the executive decision that this FYC class for L2 writers would only be offered to international visa students (Matsuda, 2008) and that the students will need to have special permission from the instructor because "that was the way it was done in the past." Since it was my first semester in a new institution, I did not offer any suggestions or critique. I started receiving emails from students who were interested in enrolling in my section. My email response prior to overriding the registration system for students to register was simply screening students for whether they self-identified as international visa students or U.S. resident ESL students (Matsuda, 2008, p. 161). If they fell into either of those categories, I usually granted their request to enroll in my section. I regularly offer both ENGL110 and ENGL120 to L2 writers on campus. I know that one section of the writing class for L2 writers each semester is not enough; therefore, I approached the writing program administrator (WPA) with the hope that we could offer two sections of the composition course for L2 writers each semester because we have a wonderful graduate student who was interested in teaching composition courses for L2 writers. The WPA agreed to offer two sections of L2 writing for one academic year. Due to budget and low enrollment issues, the graduate student came to tell me that the second L2 writing section was cancelled in the summer and was turned into a mainstream one. I was furious and disappointed because I was not informed nor asked to provide input on this decision. I was told that the enrollment number of students was low, and they had to make an executive decision. I informed them that the reason for the low enrollment was that international students were not here on campus during summer. I was disappointed because the cancellation sent a message to the assigned teaching assistant and myself that a section of L2 writing is not their main concern. If they had asked me, I would have explained that international students had to get student visa approval before they could enroll in any courses and that the enrollment of international students would increase during the first week of the semester when the students arrived to the university. I also have to be more vocal about scholarship of L2 writing in the English Department.

This incident has made me revisit the possibility of directing an L2 writing program. I approached the Bilingual/TESOL program coordinator regarding the opportunity to serve in this administrative position. The coordinator brought this issue up with the chair of the department. The chair of the department suggested that the coordinator revisit the offer letter. Within a week, the chairs of the Language, Literacy and Sociocultural Studies Department the English Department, the Bilingual/TESOL coordinator, and I had a meeting. The discussion in the meeting was mainly about the responsibility of becoming a director and how it might impact my workload in the Education department. The chairs also mentioned that if I were to be in the administrative position prior to receiving tenure, it would be better to create a memorandum of understanding (MOU) and include it as one of the documents for tenure and promotion. After the meeting, the coordinator and I discussed the possibilities and pitfalls of serving as an administrator as a pre-tenure faculty (Saenkhum, this volume). If I were to decide to do the administrative work, I would have to draft a MOU stating my roles and responsibilities between the two departments.

I faced a dilemma. If I wanted to promote and make L2 writing visible in the English Department, I would have to give up offering ENGL110 and ENGL120 for L2 writers to fulfill the role of Assistant Director of Core Writing focusing on L2 writers. The courses may be taught by other faculty members or teaching assistants (TA) who were familiar with the L2 writing scholarship. Due to the limited number of TAs in the program, only one TA had been prepared to teach the courses. Other faculty members who had training in L2 writing could be assigned to teach other courses or be on research leave. This would interrupt the offering of the courses for L2 writers. Giving up my course offerings means that L2 writers may have to enroll in composition courses that may be taught by teaching assistants who have limited-to-no-background in teaching L2 writers. On top of that, it means that I have to compromise my teaching assignment because of administrative work. I also have to revisit my work load with the Deans of Education and Arts and Sciences to negotiate my contribution as an administrator for the English Department. If I do not have such a conversation, administrative work in the English department may be perceived as service, which is considered only a fraction of my contribution by the tenure and promotion committee.

Mentoring is another aspect of work in which I put my expertise in L2 writing to use. Graduate students from both the Bilingual/TESOL and Rhetoric and Writing programs invited me to serve on their dissertation and comprehensive exam committees regarding issues in L2 writing. A few graduate students mentioned that one of the reasons they came to this institution was because they had read my publications, especially on identity construction through writing (Chamcharatsri, 2009) and emotionality and L2 writing (Chamcharatsri, 2013).

Apart from teaching and mentoring, I have been asked by many colleagues how I managed the amount of meetings I attended in both departments. Smith (2006) stated the following:

> On average, I had attended about 75 percent as many meetings as my colleagues in each department—twice over. . . . Unless I was able to do the work of two professors, I would be perceived to be subpar, even while doing more work than anyone else. (para. 14–15)

If one peeked into a monthly schedule of my position as a joint appointment for the College of Education and College of Arts and Sciences (A&S), they would find the following: two courses (ESL Composition for undergraduate international students and the Adult ESL course for graduate students), my monthly meeting schedules (four programmatic level meetings and two departmental meetings), and my committee meeting schedules (A&S: Travel funding committee; Education: Diversity Committee; University-wide service: Diversity Curriculum Subcommittee, International Student Services Committee). I occasionally had time conflicts that prevented me from attending meetings. When I was absent from the meetings, some colleagues made remarks about not seeing me in departmental meetings.

When I submitted a report of my workload in my annual review to one of my department chairs, she wrote in my annual evaluation that I should provide service to only one department; the letter stated the following:

> I would like to make special note of the fact that he provides service in two departments at UNM. It would be easy to focus his service in one part of UNM rather than another, but he appears to be a good citizen in two departments. This is commendable. (Borden, May 12, 2014).

Although I agree with Borden's recommendation for me to provide service to only one department, I feel that my lack of service in one department may result in an incomplete picture during tenure and promotion in the future. Currently, I continue to attend meetings in both programs.

## Bridging a Gap

From reflecting on my experiences as a joint appointment and discussing my position with others, I have gained insights into how to navigate academia. Having multiple interests in different disciplines can have a positive impact in the current job market as many institutions are seeking candidates who can fulfill multiple roles. For those who find themselves in joint appointment or interdisciplinary research positions, some suggestions and recommendations are provided to help ease the transition.

- Have the department or departments put all the expectations and responsibilities in writing. This suggestion was given by Paul Kei Matsuda and Jill Jeffery. In order to feel secure and show commitment in working in two departments, the document needs to indicate expectations in terms of teaching, scholarship and service between departments. This will become an important document to be included in the tenure and promotion dossier because internal tenure and promotion committee will be able to use the written document as a guideline to review the dossier. The document will also help alleviate some stress and tension of feeling overwhelmed with meetings and publications.
- Document every activity. At the Symposium on Second Language Writing (SSLW) in 2014, Christine Tardy provided a recommendation for early career L2 writing professionals that we systematically document our work-related activities. I think this is valuable advice, especially for faculty members who have joint appointments because some activities are not visible through our curriculum vitae or narrative of professional activities, such as the amount of time spent in meetings. Uncloaking the invisible work will provide the full picture of my productivity as a joint appointment, tenure-track faculty member. This documentation will help tenure and promotion committee members understand the effort the joint appointee puts into balancing the work between two departments. It will also help other faculty in both departments to see the whole picture of the joint appointment.
- Seek mentorship from both inside and outside the institution. Organizational culture plays an important role in the success of people who are working at the institution. Seeking mentors with joint appointments or interdisciplinary experience within and outside the institution is ideal because these individuals understand situations and can provide feedback and suggestions that can be adapted to a different institutional culture. In addition to outside mentors, seeking mentorship from tenured faculty members in both departments is advised because they can provide

support and offer some advice on how to navigate institutional politics.
- Strengthen interdisciplinary research agendas. In order to be visible in the departments, joint appointees can collaborate in interdisciplinary research projects with faculty members and graduate students. We can also learn more about our colleagues' research projects. Our colleagues will be able to gain more understanding of our position as a joint appointment. The collaborative projects will make my work on L2 writing more visible in different departments.

## Closing Remark: Living in the Middle

I was lucky to have supportive colleagues who understand the complexity of being a joint appointee. As I reflect on the life of a joint appointment, this is an opportunity for me to grow as an interdisciplinary scholar. Through the scholarship of L2 writing, I am fortunate to locate my ground on which to construct my scholarly identity. I have become a link between two departments to promote interdepartmental collaborations among faculty members and graduate students. This helps me expand my funds of knowledge (Moll, Amanti, Neff, & Gonzalez, 1992) beyond my graduate training and shape me to become an informed L2 scholar. Those who are finding themselves in the joint appointment position should feel honored because of their potential to grow as L2 writing specialists in the interdisciplinary world.

## References

Alsup, J. (2009). My two identities: Negotiating the challenges of being "jointly appointed." In A. Webb (Ed.), *The Doctoral Degree in English Education* (pp. 211–218). Kennesaw, GA: Kennesaw State University Press.

Chamcharatsri, P. B. (2009). Negotiating identity from auto-ethnography: Second language writers' perspectives. *Asian EFL Journal, 38,* 1–19. http://www.asian-efl-journal.com/pta_August_2009_pc.php Retrieved from http://www.asian-efl-journal.com/pta_August_2009_pc.php

Chamcharatsri, P. B. (2013). Emotionality and second language writers: Expressing fear through narrative in Thai and in English. *L2 Journal, 5*(1), 59–75.

Jacobs, D., & Micciche, L. R. (Eds.). (2003). *A way to move: Rhetoric of emotion and composition studies.* Portsmouth, NH: Boynton/Cook Publishers.

Lave, J., & Wenger, E. (1991). *Situated learning: Legitimate peripheral participation*. NY: Cambridge University Press.

Matsuda, P. K. (2006). The myth of linguistic homogeneity in U.S. college composition. *College English, 68*(6), 637–651.

Matsuda, P. K. (2013). Response: What *is* second language writing—and why does it matter? *Journal of Second Language Writing, 22*, 448–450.

Moll, L. C., Amanti, C., Neff, D., & Gonzales, N. (1992). Funds of knowledge for teaching: Using a qualitative approach to connect homes and classrooms. *Theory into practice, 31*(2), 132-141.

National Academy of Sciences (U.S.), National Academy of Engineering., & Institute of Medicine (U.S.). (2005). *Facilitating interdisciplinary research*. Washington, D.C: National Academies Press.

Smith, C. (2006). An incomplete picture. Retrieved 24 August 2014, from http://chronicle.com/article/An-Incomplete-Picture/46793

# 4 An Early-Career Second Language Writing Scholar's Professional Development in Japan: Challenges and Issues

*Atsushi Iida*

## Introduction

My professional career began in April 2011 as an Assistant Professor at a Japanese public university. It was my first full-time teaching job after completing my doctoral studies in the United States. Originally, it was not a tenure-track position; it was a five-year renewable contract position.

Before I started, I was anxious about my job in some regards. One reason was the nature of my job. I had heard that the workload at Japanese public universities was so heavy that teachers had very little time for research. I was worried about how much time I could spend on my research and how I could expand my dissertation study. Once my professional career started, I encountered the difficulty of playing multiple roles—a teacher, curriculum coordinator, and researcher—at the institution. On the one hand, it was necessary, as a faculty member, to take responsibility for institutional work; on the other hand, as an early-career researcher, I would also need to (re)build the foundation of my research and develop my scholarship. In this context, I wondered how I could develop myself as a professional. Another concern was my cultural readjustment. Since I was in a graduate program at a US university for six years, I was extremely anxious about how I could make an adjustment to a new environment.

My goal in this chapter is to provide insights for early-career scholars who are facing challenges in an unfamiliar work environment. To this end, I discuss the struggles and challenges in my professional development as an early-career second language (L2) writing scholar. This chapter describes institutional expectations in my context, identifies several issues in that context, and explores my attempts in overcoming the difficulties in developing my scholarly profile. Reflecting on my experience, I also share some strategies for professional development while balancing teaching, research, and service.

## INSTITUTIONAL EXPECTATIONS AT A JAPANESE PUBLIC UNIVERSITY

My institution is a regional, middle-sized public university in Japan, consisting of four faculties: Education, Social Information Studies, Medicine, and Science and Technology. I am not affiliated with any of them, but instead I work in the Center for Foreign Language Education where I am in charge of first- and second-year English courses. Since I am not a member of any faculty, I am in an institutionally weak position. Because my unit does not have a status as a faculty, it does not have *kyojyukai*—the monthly professor's council meeting that are central to faculty governance. I can make new proposals for new projects about English language teaching, but the final decision will be made by the dean of each faculty or the President. Also, I must obey and work, with no choice, as the President commands.

Institutional expectations comprise three areas: teaching, service, and research. The first area of the expectations is teaching. I have been teaching 5 courses, approximately 150 students, per semester. Each course has a 90 minute lesson once a week over 15 weeks. I teach first-year and second-year English courses to different groups of students including those from science, technology, engineering, education, and health sciences. These courses are part of Liberal Arts and have been designed to teach reading and listening.

The second realm of institutional expectations is service, which weighs the highest of all other duties. I have been involved in different types of service in my institution: coordinating an English curriculum; organizing faculty development (FD) seminars; designing entrance exams; and arranging study abroad programs. My major duty is to coordinate the first-year English curriculum in the School of Science and Technology. As a coordinator, I work with approximately 550 students and 20 native English speaking (NES) and Japanese teachers. I also take responsibility for managing students' placement and achievement test scores, analyzing the data, monitoring their progress in English language learning in the curriculum, and writing an annual report on teaching and research activities in my unit. Another aspect of service is to make plans and organize the FD seminar twice a year. This responsibility includes finding and contacting guest lecturers, arranging schedules with them, and hosting the events. In addition, I have designed entrance examinations every year. As a committee member of the entrance exam, I prepare a draft of the test, attend meetings twice a month during the academic year, discuss the content with other teachers, and help to develop the exam. Another type of service involves study abroad programs. I have been selected with two other colleagues from my center to help develop the programs with teachers and staff at the international office. I have explored the future collaboration with foreign universities, visited several Australian universities to discuss the potential for the student exchange agreements, and coordinated with partner institutions to build intensive English programs suitable for our students.

The third area of institutional expectations is research. However, in comparison with the four colleges of the university, research seems to be regarded as less important than teaching and service in the language center to which I am attached. This atmosphere becomes apparent in a number of ways. For example, there is a vague expectation to publish regularly, but there exists no clear policy or annual quota for scholarly activities. Also, the sabbatical system has not been established for my unit, meaning that I have no way to leave school for research during the semester. What is more, the total amount of my individual research fund is lower than that of other full-time teachers in different academic units. Amidst these incongruities in my unit, a further important task for all academics at the university is to apply for a research grant (i.e., "Grant-in-Aid for Scientific Research") provided by the Ministry of Education, Culture, Sports, Science and Technology (MEXT) and Japan Society for the Promotion of Science (JSPS) as the principal investigator. Both permanent and contract teachers in my institution are required to write and submit at least one grant proposal every year. Full-time teachers are pressured into this grant application, penalized for not submitting a proposal via reduction of twenty percent of their individual research fund. The seldom-mentioned reasons for the establishment of such a strict rule in my institution have very little to do with encouraging the development of new knowledge through research: the adoption rate of this grant proposal designed by MEXT and JSPS impacts the evaluation of public universities in Japan; and once the proposal is accepted, thirty percent of the total grant will be distributed, as indirect funding, to the institution, spent as part of the university operating budget. In such an environment, I need to keep encouraging myself to continue working on scholarly activities despite the demoralizing atmosphere of my day-to-day reality.

## CHALLENGES AND ISSUES OF AN EARLY-CAREER L2 WRITING SCHOLAR

My workload has become increasingly heavy year by year since I started working. My teaching load has not changed, but the amount of administrative work has dramatically increased. The weight of service is heavier than that of teaching and research. Along with the workload imbalance, I have found three challenges and issues in fulfilling my institutional responsibilities.

First and foremost is job insecurity. This factor affects my decisions, attitudes, and performances in various ways. For example, I always hesitate to argue my point of view and rarely speak up until called upon in meetings. When I am asked to give my opinion, I participate in the discussion maintaining a neutral position, without agreeing or disagreeing with others' opinions. I believe that it is too risky for a non-tenured or tenured-track teacher to make arguments to other tenured professors or criticize their thoughts. Due to the institutional power structure, I need to pay careful attention to every comment and action in order not to give a negative impression to other faculty members.

The issue of power relationship makes the work environment more complex . I'm the youngest full-time teacher at my institution and this age factor sometimes has negative impacts on my administrative work. My rank, age, and the length of my teaching experience impede my attendance at any important committee meetings (e.g., a hiring committee). Without any participation in such meetings, I have no chance to talk with the university executive members directly and no place to share my thoughts on the issues related to English language teaching. Unfortunately, they never understand the projects in which I am involved, what service work I am engaged in, nor how heavy my workload is. Moreover, if a full professor cannot do or does not want to do a task in my institution, it needs to be treated by other teachers and, in most cases it will be given over to younger or lower-ranking teachers. As the youngest faculty member, I must often take care of such tasks. The tenuous nature of my employment is such that I find it difficult to refuse requests from tenured professors. In other words, I have no choice to negotiate my workload. This power imbalance has given me excessive pressure and frustration.

The power relationship also makes my work as a curriculum coordinator challenging. The coordinated curriculum that I administer consists of 20 English teachers, all of whom have more teaching experience than I do. As a coordinator, I have been asked to give such veteran teachers advice, feedback and suggestions for their lessons. This is a stressful task, because I am expected to do so in a way that I maintain their face as experienced teachers and not upset them. This may be attributed to socio-cultural features in Japan. In general, Japanese are inclined to emphasize the expression of group solidarity and social harmony (Carson, 1992; Kubota, 1999) and regard the institutional success as being more important than individual accomplishments. I may subconsciously follow this way of thought and have tried my best to administer the curriculum as smoothly as possible in order for other English teachers not to get confused in their teaching. In my first two years of curriculum coordination, I always struggled with my approach to individual teachers in terms of how directly or indirectly I should express my opinions, how often I should communicate, or how closely I ought to work with the teacher. I still explore effective ways to coordinate the curriculum, but I have attempted to be friendly with them and to ask about, discuss and appreciate their situations including their impressions of students and student progress, textbooks or even problems when I see them on campus. I believe that, without their understanding and active cooperation, no English program could run smoothly. Of particular importance in successful coordination is to develop good human relationships with both full-time and part-time teachers and to gain their trust. While I understand that I should communicate with other teachers more frequently and on friendlier terms, my low self-esteem as a novice coordinator sometimes prevents me from working actively with veteran teachers.

Language issues also complicate the curriculum coordination. At my institution, there still remains a norm of native-speakerism (Holliday, 2005)—the unspoken assumption that NES teachers are superior to Japanese teachers of English in terms of English language teaching. It is represented in a strict institutional policy that specific English courses (e.g., Integrated English I) aiming specifically to develop integrated English communication ability must be taught only by NES teachers. This "native vs. non-native" dichotomy disempowers me within the institution. To make matters worse, this differentiation has produced an inequality of workload among full-time teachers. Since my institution employs Japanese as an official language, NES teachers who lack command of Japanese cannot participate in faculty meetings or understand written correspondences. In other words, a lack of Japanese proficiency makes it difficult for them to contribute to institutional work. What happens in this context is that the university executives never ask them to carry out any administrative duties that require a proficiency in Japanese; instead, those tasks will be assigned to Japanese teachers of English.

The overwhelming institutional demands also affect my level of motivation. I'm always placed in a dilemma between what I want to do and what I have to do. Although I understand that I must carry out institutional responsibilities, stress arises in my situation because I spend most of the time in my office engaging in administrative work, and I cannot do anything with my research. This reality demotivates me, and I sometimes blame myself for being unable to make any progress in my scholarly activity. These factors combine to have a negative impact on my overall performance: I often feel unsatisfied with my research, take negative attitudes toward institutional duties, and cannot concentrate on any work.

The heavy administrative workload that causes my frustration through being unable to publish makes it quite difficult for me to prepare for and obtain another job. While I am now expected to actively fulfill institutional duties, particularly in the area of service, in my current position, this does not necessarily mean that these efforts will be highly evaluated by other scholars in different institutions when I re-enter the job market in the future. In other words, my contribution to the current institution provides no leverage to be able to secure a better teaching position at another school. The fact is that publication is viewed as one of the most important requirements for academic positions in Japan and prospective applicants are required to submit three to five published papers. Without a sufficient number of refereed papers and a solid record of scholarly activities, it is extremely difficult to get a new job. So, I must handle both service and research with the same weight at the early stage of my professional career. On the one hand, this approach aims to uphold a solid record in my current institution; on the other hand, it is to prepare for my future career. In so doing, I can keep my future possibilities wide open, exploring full-time teaching positions that I feel would better suit my professional interests both inside and outside my current institution.

## STRATEGIES FOR PROFESSIONAL DEVELOPMENT

Professional development is needs-driven and varies according to each person at the different stages of his or her career (Groom, 2014). As a junior faculty member, the key for my professional development is to manage time appropriately and to balance teaching, service, and research. As discussed above, a lack of time for research is my principal problem, and I need to explore how to negotiate my workload and save time for research. There are three strategies that I have used to engage in my research activities.

First of all, I have deliberately carved out the time when I can focus on scholarly activities. I have found it very difficult to take a whole day for my research once the semester begins, so I attempt to take at least one hour every day to conduct scholarly work. This time is only for my research, and I usually work on my conference proposals and manuscripts. This daily activity not only maintains time for research, but keeps me focused on my writing in such a limited time. Regardless of the amount of daily productivity, it allows me to check the progress of my research, encourage myself to write more, and develop my self-esteem as a scholar. In so doing, I can maintain and develop my motivation for my scholarly work while negotiating with other institutional responsibilities.

In addition, I have carefully observed my context and explored how, as an L2 writing specialist, I can employ my expertise both in my individual lesson and curriculum-related work. Unfortunately there is no course related specifically to L2 writing, but I have integrated some writing activities in my reading courses. From my own past experiences and my developing viewpoint as a teacher, I believe that Japanese students need more time to develop their productive skills, which receive very little attention in secondary school education. I also realize that it takes much more time to improve L2 writing skills than others, and writing instruction requires close guidance from L2 writing experts. So, I have taught aspects of my research—poetry writing—in my classes. Doing so allows me to observe students' responses to the literacy practice, understand their attitudes toward L2 creative writing, examine effective ways for teaching poetry writing in the Japanese EFL context, and collect their written output as data, which can possibly be used for future studies. From students' perspectives, poetry writing provides an opportunity to learn a new genre in L2 writing and practically use the target language to express their emotions, thoughts or experiences (Hanauer, 2010; Iida, 2010). Combining teaching and research, even in a limited context, has helped me to gain practical and methodological insights into poetry and L2 writers and expand my research focus based on that classroom experience.

From an administrative standpoint, the exploration of issues related to the coordinated curriculum seems to provide an interesting research agenda. Nowadays, many first- and second-year college English courses in Japan have been designed and delivered through coordinated curricula. Though this is not one of my areas of expertise, my knowledge and experience of L2 writing research can be applied as a tool to empirically assess some aspects of the English curriculum. I have worked closely with my colleagues to design a case study (e.g., the effect of extensive reading on L2 reading in the EFL curriculum), to discuss the findings, and to explore more effective ways to develop and deliver the curriculum. Combining administrative duties with research allows me to take them more seriously, fostering a positive attitude even toward my institutional work while concurrently increasing my motivation to conduct research. The results gained from the study can make great contributions not only to my institution but also to the field of ELT in Japan in terms of providing an opportunity to explore and discuss what an EFL curriculum should look like.

The third strategy is to develop a network outside my institution. It is crucial for researchers, especially early-career scholars, to get to know other scholars and expand their research network in the same field, because networking can have a positive impact on scholarly activities. When I started working in Japan, I had very few connections to Japanese professors working in the same field. However, attending monthly research forums or workshops coordinated by Special Interest Groups at professional associations such as the Japan Association for Teaching, and the Japan Association of College English Teachers, and presenting my papers at conferences have allowed me to meet, get to know and have intellectual exchanges with many experienced researchers in a wide range of positions. This network has provided me with opportunities to ask for help from others, discuss personal and institutional issues, explore research topics, work on collaborative studies, gain opportunities for speaking engagements, and obtain information on job vacancies at other institutions. This type of social activity may be time-consuming, but it offers early-career scholars a great chance to recognize where to situate themselves and explore what contribution they can make in the academic community.

## Conclusion

The meaning of and approach to professional development may vary according to each scholar. My approach to professional development discussed in this chapter is just one case, and it may not be generalizable to other scholars. Of particular importance, however, is for early-career scholars to create an environment in which they can focus on their research, ask and get help from other (experienced) teachers/researchers, and share issues surrounding themselves both inside and outside their institutions.

Developing scholarship is crucial, but challenging for early-career scholars. Junior scholars are expected to engage in professional development under a lot of pressure while dealing with various personal and institutional issues such as job insecurity, power relationships, and heavy workload. While we try to understand the institutional expectations and behave appropriately in the current position, it is necessary to self-reflect and clarify where we see ourselves in the near future. I believe that exploring an ideal self, making a career plan and having clear goals help us understand what to do now and how to achieve the goals. It will also help to negotiate the work balance among teaching, service and research. In so doing, we will be able to work on professional development on a daily basis while balancing competing demands.

## NOTE

1. My school has applied a new employment policy since 2013. According to the policy, it offers a successful applicant a tenure-track position instead of a five-year contract position. Because of this change, I earned tenure in November, 2015 after having passed the tenure review process in the final year of my contract.

## REFERENCES

Carson, J. G. (1992). Becoming biliterate: First language influences. *Journal of Second Language Writing, 1,* 37–60.

Groom, N. (2014, October). *Professional development in EFL: The teacher as researcher.* Paper presented at the KOTESOL-KAFLE International Conference, Seoul, Korea.

Hanauer, D. I. (2010). *Poetry as research: Exploring second language poetry writing.* Amsterdam: John Benjamins.

Holliday, A. (2005). *The struggle to teach English as an international language.* Oxford, London.

Iida, A. (2010). Developing voice by composing haiku: A social-expressivist approach for teaching haiku writing in EFL contexts. *English Teaching Forum, 48*(1), 28–34.

Kubota, R. (1999). Japanese culture constructed by discourses: Implications for applied linguistics research and ELT. *TESOL Quarterly, 33,* 9–35.

# 5 Emergent Professional Identities of an Early Career L2 Writing Scholar

*Soo Hyon Kim*

Second language writing scholars often find academic homes within various institutional divisions. Linguistics, rhetoric and composition, English, education, TESOL, and bilingual education are some common examples. Within these various contexts, L2 writing specialists serve in a wide range of positions and fulfill the manifold needs of their institution. At some institutions, L2 writing scholars work primarily with pre-service K-12 teachers. Elsewhere, they might cover a range of linguistics and SLA courses in an applied linguistics program. Some L2 writing faculty may be called to head a TESOL program, or work with students in rhetoric and composition. We also see L2 writing specialists serve as Writing Program Administrators (WPAs) at their institution (Saenkhum, this volume) or work as university writing center directors. At institutions with a smaller number of L2 learners, L2 writing scholars may work within academic support units such as teaching and learning centers where they single-handedly perform the role of academic advisor, writing tutor, and student counselor. For some L2 writing scholars, their cross-disciplinary roles are institutionalized by means of joint appointments between different departments or programs (Chamcharatsri, this volume).

In a difficult academic climate where increasingly fewer full-time hires are being made, it is likely that scholars in other disciplines are experiencing similar pressures to perform multiple roles at their institutions. Even so, the astounding range in the departmental affiliations and positions L2 writing scholars occupy seems to imply that there is more at play than simply a hiring freeze in academia as of late. One plausible explanation may be the fundamentally issue-driven nature of our work that transcends a number of disciplines (Matsuda, 2013). Our work as L2 writing scholars is motivated by a wide variety of issues pertinent to writers, language, and texts in increasingly diverse contexts. Thus, "today, second language writing is more aptly characterized as a 'transdisciplinary field' because the intellectual work in the field transcends various disciplinary and institutional structures in addressing issues surrounding second language writing and writers" (Matsuda, 2013, p. 448). It follows that L2 writing specialists bring with them a diversity of viewpoints and identities—as well as disciplinary and institutional affiliations—from which they seek answers to their research questions.

The diversity observed in our disciplinary and institutional affiliations as L2 writing scholars may also stem from the growing scope of our field and its inquiries, as well as the resulting increase in cross-disciplinary dialogues. The research questions we seek to answer are becoming progressively more complex, as the field of L2 writing continues to expand its reach to "further embrace diversity of knowledge" (Kubota, 2013, p. 430). As Kubota aptly observes, "such inquiry would require an interdisciplinary approach, further *dislimiting* the scope of SLW" (p. 431). L2 writing scholars investigate the diverse issues surrounding L2 writing and writers in more meaningful and nuanced ways by drawing on the methodologies and wealth of knowledge accumulated in other closely related disciplines such as composition studies, education, and applied linguistics—communities who are also engaging in their own discussions of disciplinary identity and interdisiciplinarity (e.g., Bazerman, 2011; Widdowson, 2006). Scholars who self-identify with the field of L2 writing as well as scholars from other disciplinary orientations are brought together through their participation in cross-disciplinary dialogues related to L2 writing issues which, in turn, facilitates the formation and negotiation of their scholarly identities (Matsuda, 2013).

For scholars who conduct research across disciplinary boundaries, opportunities for research support and dissemination abound both inside and outside of university settings. Universities and academic departments encourage the exchange of ideas and cross-disciplinary collaboration among their faculty through various initiatives. At the University of New Hampshire, for example, faculty members are encouraged to participate in a series of workshops called the Research and Engagement Academy through which faculty from different departments form collaborative research teams. Support for cross-disciplinary research is seen beyond the university setting as well. A large number of foundations send out calls for grant proposals that involve interdisciplinary research, and many academic conferences and edited collections are also organized around interdisciplinary themes. However, it is important for our field to recognize and acknowledge the challenges that also come with this increased interest in—and push for—interdisciplinary research, especially for emerging L2 writing scholars who are striving to establish themselves within their academic institutions and the broader L2 writing community. How do early career L2 writing scholars navigate the complexities of working in an increasingly transdisciplinary academic context? Does graduate education prepare novice L2 writing scholars to meet these challenges? By reflecting on the teaching, research, and service I engage in as an early career L2 writing scholar in an English department, I contemplate how the transdisciplinary nature of our work as well as our scholarly identities as L2 writing specialists shape our workplace experiences.

## Institutional Context

The job ad for my current position at the University of New Hampshire had been for an assistant professor in English pedagogy/linguistics, and had called for applicants with a doctorate in English education or applied linguistics, with expertise in "the disciplines of English teaching (grades 5–12) and TESOL . . . [and preferably] experience teaching writing, grammar, and TESOL at the middle or high school level." The potential for productive collaborations with an exceptionally broad range of scholarship, as well as the interdisciplinary nature of the advertised position were the major draws to my job. When I accepted the job offer, it was fairly easy to anticipate some of the upcoming changes that would come from moving to and settling in a different state, city, and local community; yet, I underestimated the adjustments I would have to make in the process of transitioning to life as a faculty member in a large English department within a different institutional context.

The most conspicuous difference I noticed upon starting my new job was at the university level. Throughout my years as a master's and doctoral student at two large public research universities, I had grown accustomed to their large student populations and the remarkable level of diversity in both their student bodies and programs. My new academic home, a mid-sized flagship state university with a strong commitment to regional undergraduate education, was different on every front: university mission, student body, and culture.

Within this broader context, the most significant changes that occurred in my daily interactions were at the departmental level. The English department at UNH is one of the largest departments on campus with 38 tenure track faculty and 24 lecturers offering multiple undergraduate and graduate majors. What sets it apart, other than its size, is the constellation of programs housed under its roof, brought together by an appreciation of the English language. It is home to five undergraduate majors in English, English literature, journalism, English teaching, and linguistics and offers graduate programs in literature, composition, creative writing, teaching, and language and linguistics. The University Writing Program and the ESL Institute are run out of the English department as well. While these programs are designed to work together within a single department to encourage communication and mutual reinforcement, the immense size of the department and the large number of faculty members, programs, and courses can present challenges for newly hired faculty members who are just starting to learn how to integrate themselves into the life of the department and university. In the following sections, I describe some of my personal challenges and triumphs in teaching, research, and service during my first few years as an early career scholar.

## Teaching: Facilitating Cross-disciplinary Dialogues

The courses I routinely teach at my institution include upper-level courses in TESOL Theory and Methods; ESL Curriculum Design, Materials, and Assessment; English Grammar; and Issues in Second Language Writing. Unlike other institutional contexts in which these courses may be taught within a comprehensive TESOL or applied linguistics curriculum, at UNH, these courses typically attract students who are primarily invested in affiliate disciplines but are interested in issues relevant to TESOL and L2 writing. I offer these courses through several curricular paths: as required courses for the TESOL minor program I direct, or in the case of English Grammar, as a requirement for K-12 teacher certification. The courses also serve as electives for linguistics, foreign languages, and international affairs undergraduate majors and minors, or graduate students in English education or composition studies. In addition, in-service K-12 teachers occasionally take these courses for professional development, as do ESL Institute lecturers, or sometimes, foreign language teaching assistants. Together, these students represent a great spectrum of educational backgrounds, experiences, motivations, goals, and expectations that come together through an interest in L2 writing and/or TESOL issues.

I had not given much thought to the potential difficulties involved in bringing together students from various majors and academic levels to study issues surrounding L2 writing, until it resulted in an embarrassing episode during my first semester at UNH. My senior colleagues wanted to make sure that my first semester would be a smooth transition and, therefore, had assigned Issues in Second Language Writing as one of the courses I would teach. As the first week of classes slowly approached and official class rosters were made available, I noticed that I only had three students enrolled. Having heard that most upper-level courses enroll somewhere between 15 to 25 students, I contacted the Registrar's office and a senior colleague thinking surely there was a mistake. What I did not realize at the time was that, staying true to its transdisciplinary nature, the L2 writing course was cross-listed as an elective, and not established as a core course in any major curriculum. Thus, in order to ensure adequate enrollment, it had traditionally been offered every third semester in the spring, after various forms of advertisement.

While identifying and creating a community of students interested in L2 writing may be a unique challenge in my teaching context, the greater challenge of teaching a diverse student body, both in terms of their majors and academic levels, has been in responding to students' needs and expectations. For example, graduate students in composition studies often want more in-depth discussions of theory, while undergraduate students and in-service teachers look forward to more hands-on, immediately applicable strategies for working with L2 writers. I have received feedback from undergraduate students that the theoretical readings are too dense and overwhelming, while some graduate students have commented that the structured think-pair-share sequence of class discussions remind them too much of high school.

While I have sought to address these student concerns out of a genuine desire to improve my teaching, as a pre-tenured faculty member, the thought of negative student evaluations and their repercussions has also weighed heavily on my mind. I have learned to channel this apprehension into looking for productive solutions and pushing myself to think more explicitly about my course objectives, consider students' goals and expectations, and solicit constructive feedback. For example, instead of giving undergraduate and graduate students identical assignments that only vary in length, I have designed projects specifically for graduate students that could potentially lead to publications, and that would challenge them to situate their work within the larger body of scholarship in TESOL and L2 writing. Also, I remind myself and my students that the diversity of experiences and knowledge students bring to class is, without a doubt, a great resource for all class participants involved. I often encourage students to actively listen and engage each other in dialogue. I also share student reflections from previous semesters, in which students noted that hearing viewpoints that were drastically different from their own helped them critically examine some of their long-held beliefs and assumptions.

## Research: Gaining Breadth and Depth in Scholarship

Establishing a transdisciplinary research identity as an L2 writing scholar can be difficult when working in a department that is based on a different discipline than the one in which your work is primarily situated, or the one in which you received your graduate training. This is frequently the case for L2 writing scholars who are the sole L2 writing expert at their institutions. I fortunately have a senior colleague in composition studies who is an established expert in L2 writing and with whom I can share ideas about teaching and research surrounding L2 writing issues. Nevertheless, my first couple of years at UNH introduced several changes I needed to adapt to as I transitioned from being a doctoral student in a second language studies doctoral program to an L2 writing scholar and new faculty member within a larger, more academically diverse department.

On the one hand, having come from an intensely focused doctoral program, it was fascinating to overhear hallway conversations quoting Shakespeare and Milton. Yet, on the other, I found that even answering well-meaning questions about my area of research had suddenly become fraught with difficulty. I recall feeling flustered while introducing myself at a joint meeting between English and Education faculty during my first semester at UNH. As we went around the table introducing ourselves, I started feeling an increasing sense of unease. My first instinct was that I should introduce myself as a linguistics faculty member since my formal position was within that program, but then I wondered if that might give the impression that I was a theoretical linguist. I asked myself if I should instead talk about my commitment to second language writing and TESOL, or if I should describe my involvement with English teaching majors. These flurries of thoughts were still running through my mind when it became my turn to introduce myself, and I ended up stumbling through an unsatisfactory introduction that I was a linguistics faculty member in English that teaches the required grammar course for English teaching majors. While my discomfort may not have been particularly noticeable to my colleagues, I came away from that meeting constantly playing back that moment, upset that I had not been able to truly represent the work that I do and am passionate about. I also anxiously wondered if that blunder might have cost me future collaborations and opportunities with Education faculty.

While this experience heightened my awareness about the way I position my scholarly work and identity inside and outside of my department, I have come to realize that this positioning is not only a matter of coming up with the perfect self introduction. Clearly communicating that I am, in fact, an applied linguist and L2 writing scholar, and not a theoretical linguist has real repercussions for my professional advancement, especially related to issues of tenure and promotion. Within the first few weeks of starting my job and attending new faculty orientations, several questions emerged to which few people had answers: Would my promotion and tenure case be based on the department criteria established for linguistics or English teaching? How would I make the case that my work has been published in academic journals that are well respected within the field of L2 writing? Would I have the opportunity to provide input on possible outside reviewers for my tenure case? Would these reviewers be academics in linguistics, applied linguistics, education, or composition? While my position as an assistant professor in English pedagogy/linguistics was created to enable interdisciplinary work, it seemed that the parameters of what that entails needed far more definition. As I began to learn that it was crucial for me to proactively seek clarifications to these questions and negotiate expectations regarding promotion and tenure, I requested meetings with my department chair and senior colleagues in linguistics and English teaching to clarify promotion and tenure criteria. Recently, I have been initiating more conversations with colleagues about my research projects as a way to solicit feedback and also further establish my scholarly identity within the department.

Over the past few years, I have also begun to engage in more introspection about my place beyond the English department and within the larger community of L2 writing scholars. As I started mapping out my research agenda, I quickly realized that the limited number of years I had for building a tenure case would require some measured decisions. The challenge would be in making sure that each of those decisions would balance the breadth of my different areas of scholarship and the depth of my specific area of expertise in L2 writing.

One particularly difficult decision I had to make after my first year at UNH was initiating the exciting but laborious process of conducting foundational research in a new area on which I wanted to build expertise. Starting a new research project on mixed methods methodology required endless summer hours spent reading research articles, gathering preliminary data, and preparing to present at the Mixed Methods International Research Association conference. While this was undoubtedly a project that I felt passionate about, I had to overcome my initial fear and hesitation about dedicating the majority of my efforts to starting this project. I knew that doing so would inevitably mean time away from my other research interests, as well as a summer without any tangible results or publications which, in the short term, could possibly put my annual performance review at risk.

The choices I make about conference proposals and attendance also collectively shape my research narrative and scholarly presence in the field. Several considerations factor into these decisions: my current research projects and their intended audience, scheduling conflicts between conferences, availability of financial resources, and my ability to compensate for time spent away from teaching, grading, and student advising. For these reasons, saying yes to certain opportunities means saying no to others. In the past years, attending both the American Association of Applied Linguistics (AAAL) and TESOL has been fairly convenient in terms of travel and expenses due to the consecutive hosting of both in the same geographical location. Attending these conferences, however, has sometimes meant forgoing participation at the Conference on College Composition and Communication (CCCC) due to scheduling conflicts. However, other factors such as the time and funds available in a given semester also impact decisions about participating in conferences such as the National Council of Teachers of English (NCTE) or the Second Language Research Forum (SLRF). Similarly, given the lengthy and involved process of publishing research articles, writing and submitting manuscripts also require informed decisions. Engaging in multiple disciplinary dialogues through publications is no small feat; it involves knowing which discipline your manuscript best aligns with, selecting a well-respected academic journal within that discipline that will reach your intended audience and learning how to write according to their disciplinary conventions (Ruecker, this volume).

## Service: Finding Meaningful Professional Development

Unlike the research and teaching we do as early career scholars, the service we provide to our institutions and profession seems to be an area of work we seldom discuss. The most common advice that I have received when it comes to service is to "get involved; be a good citizen" and to "say no." The conflicting nature of this advice is understandable. While our service and leadership as faculty make meaningful contributions to our institutions, they require much time, which is a scarce resource in academia. Moreover, L2 writing scholars are frequently invited to serve in numerous capacities at our respective institutions due to our transdisciplinary work and positions. At my institution, I serve as an academic advisor for undergraduate and graduate students in linguistics and English teaching. Also, as one of the few faculty members at my institution whose work directly concerns language learners, I am called on to advise incoming international students, or head college committees that grant scholarships to international students. I am occasionally asked to provide faculty development workshops on strategies for working with ESL students as well.

One of the best pieces of advice I have received about handling these service requests is that, when possible, I should volunteer for and stick to service missions that I am passionate about. By doing so, service to the department, university, or profession would not be onerous, time-consuming tasks, but fulfilling projects that can also relate to my professional development. For instance, I distinctly remember a rewarding experience serving on a graduate dissertation fellowship committee for the TESOL International Association. While I did have to invest a great amount of time in reading through student application essays and faculty recommendation letters, it was gratifying to be able to give back to the profession by serving on the committee, especially as I had previously benefited from the fellowship as a graduate student. In addition, this service mission gave me a glimpse of the latest research being produced by emerging scholars in TESOL and also helped me become familiar with the ways academic advisors wrote letters of recommendation, a fairly new genre of writing I needed to learn as a new faculty member. Through this experience, I was able to take up both pieces of advice: I was serving a mission I felt passionate about, and I was also keeping up with my own professional development as an early career L2 writing scholar.

## Professional Development in L2 Writing: A Concerted Effort

At the first major disciplinary conference I attended after starting my job, I found that I was not entirely alone in struggling to navigate the complexities of being a transdisciplinary scholar in a new institutional context. Newly minted-PhDs who had recently landed their first positions gathered here and there to swap stories about their new institutional homes, most of them relaying their surprise at the different institutional cultures and expectations they encountered in their new positions.

Doctoral programs can take small but significant steps to better prepare these early L2 writing scholars to join an increasingly diverse and transdisciplinary work setting. One way would be to help raise students' awareness of various types of institutions in addition to their missions and student bodies. A considerable number of novice L2 writing scholars come from doctoral programs intensely focused on a certain area of study, for example composition studies or applied linguistics. Yet, due to the issue-driven, transdisciplinary nature of our work in L2 writing, these novice scholars often transition into faculty positions that are based in different disciplinary contexts. To prepare novice scholars for this change, it would help for doctoral programs to create opportunities for students to take coursework outside of their core requirements and develop cognate areas, in addition to acquiring disciplinary knowledge in their specific area of work. As a doctoral student, I took courses in literacy development in the education department, and taught both ESL and K-12 teacher education courses. I also participated in research activities at the writing center run by the rhetoric and composition program, and stayed engaged with local professional organizations. Looking back, while the core graduate courses I took in my doctoral program undoubtedly helped build a foundation in my primary areas of TESOL and applied linguistics, it was these additional paths that I willfully explored outside my program that helped broaden my perspectives and prepared me for the challenges of working in a multidisciplinary English department.

Early career L2 writing scholars, our academic institutions, and the broader L2 writing community all need to engage in more introspection on the complexities involved in performing and supporting transdisciplinary scholarly identities. Graduate students and early career L2 writing scholars could benefit from reflecting on how we position ourselves and our scholarly work: which disciplinary traditions do we pull from and align with, and how do we engage with those academic communities? How do these choices shape our professional identities as well as our day to day research, teaching, and service? Writing this chapter, for example, has helped me become more aware of the complexities involved in my professional identity, and how it shapes the choices I make and the impact I have within my institutional and scholarly communities. These discussions are greatly needed at the institutional and disciplinary level as well. While institutions increasingly seek faculty with interdisciplinary experience and expertise, institutional discussions regarding the parameters of these interdisciplinary hires are sorely lagging. Explicit disciplinary dialogues on professional development in L2 writing such as those in this collection and those that took place at the Symposium on Second Language Writing 2014 can help strengthen infrastructures that allow emerging L2 writing scholars to thrive in the transdisciplinary work we do at our respective institutions and within the larger L2 writing community.

## REFERENCES

Bazerman, C. (2011). Standpoints: The disciplined interdisciplinarity of writing studies. *Research in the Teaching of English, 46*(1), 8–21.

Kubota, R. (2013). Dislimiting second language writing. *Journal of Second Language Writing, 22,* 430–431.

Matsuda, P. (2013). Response: What is second language writing—And why does it matter? *Journal of Second Language Writing, 22,* 448–450.

Widdowson, H. (2006). Viewpoint: Applied linguistics and interdisciplinarity. *International Journal of Applied Linguistics, 16*(1), 93–96.

# 6 Publishing as an Early Second Language Writing Scholar: Developing an Academic Voice and Navigating Disciplinary Expectations

*Todd Ruecker*

As a junior scholar, I have faced conflicting messages in regard to publication. One of my graduate professors made it clear that graduate students shouldn't try to publish, saying that we had much to learn before we could make substantive contributions to the field. Others told me that I should have a few publications in press or published before I entered the job market. Recognizing the value of publishing in terms of contributing to the field and for my career trajectory, I opted for the latter approach and actively published as a graduate student. However, this journey has presented a variety of challenges, both in terms of developing the voice suitable for academic publication and in terms of navigating different disciplinary expectations.

Casanave and Vandrick's 2003 collection *Writing for Scholarly Publication* is one of the few books that has helped make the publication process transparent, detailing the challenges both new and experienced scholars face in publishing. In one of the chapters, Matsuda (2003) mentioned the prejudice from some people in the field who held the view that graduate students shouldn't rush to publish in part because of the assumption that publishing took time away from reading widely. In another chapter, Braine (2003) narrated his experience trying to publish his first article, dealing with reviewers who were annoyed by his "American writing style" and criticized Braine for not actually engaging in research. Lee and Norton (2003) discussed a variety of obstacles that graduate students attempting to publish face, including envisioning academic audiences, choosing the right venue, and translating their work into a book.

While authors in Casanave and Vandrick (2003) examined different publishing challenges faced by both emerging and established scholars, they did not deal extensively with the specific challenges faced by L2 writing scholars publishing across different disciplines—with the exception of Braine who did briefly compare his experiences attempting to publish in composition and applied linguistics journals. In an article published in *Modern Language Journal,* Silva and Leki (2004) provided some insight into some of the differences between the two disciplines I have typically published in as an L2 writing scholar: applied linguistics and composition studies (see Table 1).

Table 1. Differences between applied linguistics and composition studies (Silva & Leki, 2004)

|  | **Applied Linguistics** | **Composition Studies** |
| --- | --- | --- |
| **Ontology** | Realist | Relativist |
| **Epistemology** | Objectivist | Subjectivist |
| **Methodology** | Empirical | Hermeneutic/Dialectic |
| **Axiology** | Explanation of language phenomena | Changing attitudes and behaviors of writers |
| **Scope** | International | National/Monocultural |

While this contrast is helpful to understanding some of the differences between applied linguistics and composition studies, I found these divides to not be as rigid as this table makes them appear. For instance, some scholars in applied linguistics have advocated for a stronger sociopolitical perspective that moves toward the relativist end of the spectrum (e.g., Casanave, 2003a) which conflicts with the expected realist ontology as described in Table 1. In terms of methodology, we have seen composition scholars (e.g., Haswell, 2005; Johanek, 2000) critique their discipline for failing to value and engage in empirical work. The formation of the transnational standing group at the Conference on College Composition and Communication and the work by scholars like Donahue (2009) have helped push for the internationalization of writing studies. Despite some disciplinary shifts initiated by these and other scholars, the binaries still persist. For scholars embedded in the professional work of multiple disciplines, a significant challenge is the initial need to be aware of these disciplinary differences, differences that I have had to navigate while writing for scholarly audiences that did not always possess such a transdisciplinary orientation.

While navigating multiple disciplines, I have faced the additional challenge of writing for a variety of audiences in a particular discipline who have different disciplinary perspectives. As Hyland (2004) noted, a discipline is not one monolithic community but rather is:

> composed of individuals with diverse experiences, expertise, commitments and influence. There are considerable variations in the extent to which members identify with their myriad goals, methods and beliefs, participate in their diverse activities, and identify themselves with their conventions histories or values. (p. 9)

From the more straightforward process of identifying journals to the more complex process of negotiating the expectations of diverse readers, I have dealt with a variety of considerations when attempting to publish. Nonetheless, I have long known that publication is generally treated as a central way to develop my identity (Casanave, 2003b; Ivanič, 1998) and the most valued part of my work in terms of obtaining a position and achieving tenure at a research institution.

This chapter explores the way I, as an early career L2 writing scholar, have faced the challenge of developing an academic voice and the additional complexity of navigating different disciplines' expectations while completing a doctoral program and then working toward tenure at a research university.

## Early Article Publishing Experiences: Struggling to Develop an Academic Voice While Understanding Audience Expectations

While my formal academic training was primarily situated in English studies and composition, my earliest attempts at publication focused on TESOL and applied linguistics journals. Both attempts, one pedagogically-focused and one research-focused, emerged from classes in which my professors encouraged us to write for publication and from my interest in being a transdisciplinary L2 writing scholar. With this goal in mind, I set out from the beginning to target specific journals and their audiences while writing.

For an article based on a project I conducted with English L1 and L2 speakers in Chile, I wrote for a pedagogically-oriented journal targeted toward TESOL professionals. I thought that the shorter nature of the articles and restrictions on the number of external sources would help make the process easier than trying to publish in a research-oriented journal. I also thought that the pedagogical orientation of the journal would use a less formal writing style than a more research-oriented journal. After a few months of working on this article for a class project and revising in response to feedback provided by my professor, I went ahead and submitted, confident that I was writing something well-suited for the journal.

However, I quickly learned that submitting the piece was only the beginning of a year-long process that involved several rounds of revision. While one reviewer was initially quite positive about my draft, another continually raised concerns not only with the content but also with the style of my writing. Comments on my initial submission included the following:

> This is an interesting but not very well written article. The issues raised are relevant in many higher education contexts throughout the world and most readers would find something of interest and relevance in the article if it were presented as a research paper and not as a personal account of a noteworthy project. In order to salvage the article, it needs to be restructured, refocussed and edited with due academic rigour. . . .
>
> . . . The Design section is wordy and fails to provide an accurate description of the project. How many participants were

involved? How many speakers of English/Spanish? How were the participants selected? How were the groups formed? What topics were chosen to write about and why? How were the peer-review sessions structured, observed, etc.?

Some of the reviewer's critique of my writing style is likely attributed to the fact that I was a novice scholar developing an academic voice. I believe it was also complicated by the fact that I was writing for a disciplinary audience I was less familiar with. However, there appeared to be other issues at play than writing style. Neither my MA program nor the PhD program I was in at the time offered courses in empirical methods; in general, my academic background was more oriented towards hermeneutic/dialectic methods. As the reviewer noted, this piece read more like a "personal account" and included irrelevant methodological details.

Based on the reviewers' feedback, I revised the piece extensively and shared it with my mentor before resubmitting. After a six-week review period, I received similar comments from the same reviewer, who wrote:

> There are long and convoluted sentences which need to be untangled and made clear. The first paragraph of the introduction should be shortened: It should include details of the project only and there is no need for personal narrative.

I was clearly struggling with the writing style expected by this reviewer and presumably the journal. While my reading of book chapters and journal articles in rhetoric and composition gave me the impression that personal narratives are appropriate for academic writing, my audience in this case had different expectations. I had to go through two more rounds of revision.

During the ongoing revision process, my introduction went through several iterations, removing what the reviewer considered extraneous (and sometimes personal) details. The following are three versions of my opening sentence:

> **Original Submission:** "Before starting a doctoral program in rhetoric and writing studies with a focus on L2 writing, I spent seven months interning and teaching for a program designed to promote English learning in Chile."

> **Revision 1:** "In this article, I draw on data collected during a pilot project conducted at a Chilean university to discuss the rationale behind dual-language cross-cultural peer review and why this type of peer review is an improvement on traditional peer review."
>
> **Revision 2:** "In this article, I explain the rationale behind dual-language, cross-cultural peer review and why this type of peer review is an improvement on traditional peer review models."

Similarly, from the time of my first submission to the final submission, I cut the method section by half, reducing the amount of personal and contextual detail to focus just on the study itself. Here's an early and later example of one part of the method:

> **Original Submission:** "The students read the papers at the beginning of the meetings, providing written comments on both the feedback sheets and the papers. They then took turns to discuss their comments orally. The groups met individually in a small conference room at the university and sessions lasted about an hour. The discussions were recorded and copies were made of the commented papers and completed feedback sheets."
>
> **Final Manuscript:** "Meeting for about an hour, the participants exchanged papers, read the papers written by students from a different country, provided written comments on both the papers and a feedback sheet, and then discussed their comments orally."

Despite the ongoing difficulties I faced in meeting the reviewers' expectations, my careful and persistent attention to the reviewers' concerns paid off: The challenging reviewer recommended acceptance and the piece was published. Throughout this process, I was encouraged by the fact that the journal editor continued to invite me to revise, something that my mentor had told me signaled that the editor was interested in my work. From the beginning, my mentor had encouraged me to be persistent and was confident that I would be able to publish the piece.

My road toward publication continued with a second piece that emerged out of a critical race theory seminar I took during my doctoral studies. This project involved recognizing how critical race theory and rhetorical studies could provide a new way to examine and deconstruct the native/nonnative English speaker (NES/NNES) hierarchy in English language teaching (ELT). Although I planned to draw on theories of rhetoric in the article, I targeted an applied linguistics journal for publication because the primary focus of this piece was not on writing or writing instruction but the way language positioned language teachers. Unlike the Chilean piece, it was a critical article not based on an empirical study, a choice that would present challenges.

At this point in my doctoral studies, I had started to make connections with other scholars at conferences, something my mentor encouraged me to do. Perhaps stemming from my ongoing research interest in peer review, I grew increasingly aware that I needed to seek feedback beyond my mentor to gain different perspectives on my work. So in addition to receiving feedback from multiple professors in my program, who were primarily situated in rhetoric and composition, I sought out feedback from a World Englishes scholar who had published on the problems with the native speaker standard. After eight months of writing and revising based on feedback from three different people, I submitted the manuscript.

After six weeks, I received a cursory reply that, because the article was not empirical, the editors would not send it out for review. I was surprised because I knew composition journals and applied linguistics journals both published theoretical work and that this particular journal's aims and scope description encouraged publication of diverse theoretical and methodological approaches.

Having learned the value of persistence from mentors and from a session on publishing I attended at a conference, I revised this piece and submitted it to another journal. Since I had a personal connection to the topic I was writing about, I began with a short personal narrative to engage the readers and build my ethos: "In Summer 2002, I was working at a hotel in Alaska with people from all over the world when my interest in English language teaching (ELT) was sparked." While this approach might have gotten more traction with a composition audience, it was not well received by one reviewer who wrote, "The writing style is subjective and, as such, unlikely to appeal to scholars. The end result is a choppy commentary that reads like a journal entry by an individual relatively new to the field." Upon reflection, I should have learned my lesson from my experience with my previous publication to avoid an overly personal tone in academic writing for certain disciplinary audiences. I was still struggling to find my academic voice, something complicated by the fact that I was writing for an applied linguistics audience with which I had yet to gain more familiarity. Fortunately, I was given an opportunity to revise and resubmit.

While discouraged by the negative comments, I sought solace in the fact that I sounded "relatively new" when I was, in fact, new. I revised the piece substantially and sent it to a few colleagues and friends for feedback before resubmitting. My new opening was much less personal: "This article offers a new direction for studying native speakerism by arguing that English Language Teaching (ELT) scholars should draw more broadly on theories of difference developed by race theorists." I made a variety of other changes throughout to build my academic ethos, such as adding a section focused on defining terms relevant to my argument and adding citations to defend my use of online discourses in making an argument. My effort paid off, and the piece was accepted after another round of minor revision. After about two years from the initial submission, it appeared in print.

Through these early experiences involving multiple rounds of revision and long periods of waiting, I learned that the process can be long and tedious, that I need to be more conscious of my writing style when writing for different disciplinary audiences, that I should provide sufficient but not extraneous detail about my study design when publishing from empirical work, and that persistence was an important part of publishing successfully. These early article publishing experiences also showed me the value of transdisciplinary work (e.g., new knowledge developed through synthesizing knowledge from different fields), while continuing to illustrate that publishing this type of work can present challenges beyond simply the novice writer struggling to find their academic voice.

## Academic Book Publishing: Meeting the Expectations of Different Disciplinary Audiences

Upon taking a new job at the University of New Mexico, I quickly learned that an academic monograph is the gold standard for tenure in my school's English Department (as it is at many research university English departments). Conversely, a colleague in L2 writing whose tenure home at UNM was in the College of Education learned quickly that he should focus on publishing articles (see Chamcharatsri, this collection, for more on his experiences navigating the expectations of two departments).

I began the book process by approaching acquisitions editors for publishers at the Conference on College Composition and Communication (CCCC). Since my dissertation was completed in a rhetoric and composition doctoral program and primarily targeted a composition audience, I felt that it would be more viable to publish with a composition press. I began with a well known, albeit traditional, composition press that had recently shown an interest in language diversity, publishing a collection by a well-known L2 writing scholar. The editor quickly told me that they weren't interested in work focused on high school writing instruction. This indicated that I may have trouble finding interest in work focused in part on high school writing instruction at a conference largely focused on postsecondary writing. Fortunately, the issue was resolved easily: The second editor I talked with was much more open to and interested in the project. Encouraged by both the editor's interest and my own interest in books his press had published, I decided that this publisher would be a good fit for my work. Although it is an accepted practice to submit a prospectus to multiple publishers, I was starting the book process early enough (in terms of my tenure clock) that I felt confident submitting my prospectus to this publisher only.

Before I submitted the prospectus to the publisher, I shared my materials with colleagues at other institutions who had gone through the book publishing process and who were familiar with my work. My composition colleague found an engaging narrative missing in my initial attempt at a book introduction. She explained this in her feedback: "But while the intro should definitely preview the book to some extent, you also want it to provide that compelling hook." Later in her comments, she followed up with a more extended explanation:

> I like reading the profiles of the students and this summary about how you came to meet them, etc. But I'm still missing some of the energy I'm sure (!) you have around the project. What struck you with these students about their situations? What motivated you to think that they could help you to explore the questions you've defined in relation to the issues you

want to explore/the questions you've asked? I feel like a need for some more oomph here.

In contrast to the concerns raised by the reviewer when I attempted a more narrative approach in an applied linguistics article, now a more composition-situated reader was suggesting a narrative full of personal details to satisfy a composition audience's expectations. I revised this introduction several times, repeatedly receiving feedback from both this colleague and my mentor that it still sounded like a dissertation. Here are three versions of my opening sentences, which each led into very different opening sections:

> **Revision 1:** "This project arose from two areas that have traditionally been overlooked in composition studies: Writing that students do before their arrival on the campus of a four-year college or university, as well as the challenges beyond the classroom that minority students, specifically Latina/o students, face beyond the institution as they learn how to write in academic environments."
>
> **Revision 5:** "I asked every high school and college teacher the obvious question in a study focused on student writers transitioning to college: 'Do you feel that students in high school are getting the writing instruction they need to be prepared for college?'"
>
> **Final Version:** "In El Paso, Texas, the largest port of entry from Mexico into the United States, transition is a way of life. Every day, people line up on the arched bridges spanning the Rio Grande, coming by car, bike, or on foot to the United States to shop, study, or work."

Due in part to my early publishing experiences, where I faced reviewers who likely would have preferred Revision 1 as an opening to an article, I was finding it difficult to engage in the more narrative-style writing present in the Final Version. However, focused feedback and a willingness to revise aggressively while exploring a variety of options through brainstorming activities eventually helped me to write an introductory chapter that didn't sound too much like a dissertation.

In a more recent co-edited book project focused on the transitions of resident multilingual students from high school to college (one that is being published by the applied linguistics strand of a publisher), I confronted the challenge of interdisciplinary audiences more directly than I did in my initial book project. As editors, we sought from the beginning to bring in scholars from both composition and applied linguistics and had to decide between composition- and applied linguistics-oriented publishers. We ended up with the latter. However, the editor raised concerns about our proposed title, because it used the term *resident multilingual,* which is preferred in composition circles. The editor thought it sounded like an insider term and suggested *linguistic minority,* which is more common in applied linguistics (e.g., Kanno & Harklau, 2011). One of our peer reviewers raised concerns about "specialized terminology" in one of the chapters, although that term (literacy sponsorship) was widely understood and used by composition scholars.

As we provided feedback to authors, we faced the additional challenge of considering the terminology and theories they used, and how to make them accessible yet interesting to audiences in two distinct fields. We grappled with differences in chapter structuring, with authors more situated in applied linguistics organizing their chapters in the traditional IMRAD (Introduction, Methodology, Results, Analysis, and Discussion) format while the composition pieces used a variety of organizational structures.

## FINAL THOUGHTS AND RECOMMENDATIONS

From my experiences, it's clear that many of the challenges I faced in attempting to publish as an early career scholar were simply learning how to write for an academic audience. I was fortunate to have reviewers and editors who were patient with me as I was given the opportunity to revise multiple times. However, I believe that the challenges I faced as a novice academic writer during early publishing attempts were further complicated because I was navigating different epistemological and methodological terrains than ones in which I was trained. While the journey toward publishing as an early career scholar is never easy, and is perhaps even more complicated for an L2 writing scholar publishing across disciplinary boundaries, there are a few things I have learned along the way that have helped:

*Audiences in different disciplines (and even within a discipline) have different expectations.* Having taught in a writing program with a curriculum that emphasizes different discourse communities, I recognized that different disciplines would have different conventions and that each discipline contained a variety of audiences (Beaufort, 2007; Hyland, 2004); however, it was difficult to translate this recognition into practice. For example, even after a reviewer on my first article submission gave a clear message that starting with a personal narrative was unacceptable in an academic article, I repeated this strategy when I submitted a later manuscript for publication. Because of these experiences, I initially wrote a book introduction that was formal and lacking in narrative qualities and might have appealed to one of these reviewers on my early pieces; however, another colleague thought that I needed to bring more narrative in to engage readers.

In order to navigate these different expectations, I learned that it is valuable to create a national network of mentors and that conferences are an important place where emerging scholars can meet experienced mentors. I believe seeking feedback before submission has played an important role in getting my submissions through the first gatekeeper, the journal or book editor. Since my first publication, I have rarely sent anything out for review without first seeking feedback from someone familiar with my target audience and with whom I had developed a professional relationship.

*It takes time to write and publish.* As I recounted above, my first publication took over two years to appear in print. I began submitting manuscripts in the second year of my PhD program, which was a good time for me because I had the time to build up my knowledge of L2 writing as well as composition studies, fields I did not study extensively during my master's program. For students better prepared at the master's level, this time may come earlier. I always encourage my students to read well beyond what they are doing in their courses in order to build up the confidence to submit something for publication in the first few years of their doctoral program.

*Persistence and willingness to engage in extensive revision, often in the face of discouraging comments, is important.* While some reviewers may sense that an author is a new scholar when reading a manuscript and may soften their criticism of the work, others, like some of the early reviewers I encountered, may not hold back on negative and potentially hurtful feedback. Multiple reviewers told me I clearly did not know the writing conventions expected in academic journals. While it would have been easy to walk away in disappointment or complain about unreasonable reviewers, I persisted, eventually winning over the most skeptical reviewers as I engaged in extensive revision processes that helped me develop my scholarly voice. During this time, I took to heart the words I heard from a more established scholar who told me that the people who try the most to publish, publish the most. Along with persistence, I have always demonstrated a willingness to take reviewer feedback seriously and to revise extensively. On my earlier publications, I would always seek feedback from mentors or colleagues to see if I was addressing reviewer feedback sufficiently.

Publishing as an early career scholar is a challenge, one that is more difficult for L2 writing scholars who engage in transdisciplinary work. Learning more about different discourse communities, leaving plenty of time for the publication process, and being persistent while revising carefully and often extensively are just a few ways that can help one navigate this process successfully. As they overcome these challenges with a variety of strategies, early L2 writing scholars will learn one of the most valuable parts of publishing as part of a transdisciplinary field: The ability to engage in discussions across disciplines. This kind of transdisciplinary engagement has greatly enhanced my understanding of the nature of L2 writing and writers.

## References

Beaufort, A. (2007). *College writing and beyond: A new framework for university writing instruction.* Logan, UT: Utah State University Press.

Braine, G. (2003). Negotiating the gatekeepers: The journey of an academic article. In C. P. Casanave & S. Vandrick (Eds.), *Writing for scholarly publication: Behind the scenes in language education* (pp. 87–108). Mahwah, NJ: Lawrence Erlbaum Associates.

Casanave, C. P. (2003a). Looking ahead to more sociopolitically-oriented case study research in L2 writing scholarship: (But should it be called "post-process"?). *Journal of Second Language Writing, 12*(1), 85–102.

Casanave, C. P. (2003b). Narrative braiding; Constructing a multistrand portrayal of self as writer. In C. P. Casanave & S. Vandrick (Eds.), *Writing for scholarly publication: Behind the scenes in language education* (pp. 157–74). Mahwah, NJ: Lawrence Erlbaum Associates.

Casanave, C. P., & Vandrick, S. (Eds.). (2003) *Writing for scholarly publication: Behind the scenes in language education.* Mahwah, NJ: Lawrence Erlbaum Associates.

Donahue, C. (2009). " Internationalization" and Composition Studies: Reorienting the Discourse. *College Composition and Communication,* 61(2), 212–243.

Horner, B., Lu, M. Z., Royster, J. J., & Trimbur, J. (2011). Language difference in writing: Toward a translingual approach. *College English,* 73(3), 303–321.

Hyland, K. (2004). *Disciplinary discourses: Social interactions in academic writing.* Ann Arbor, MI: University of Michigan Press.

Ivanič, R. (1998). *Writing and identity: The discoursal construction of identity in academic writing.* Philadelphia, PA: John Benjamins.

Johanek, C. (2000). Composing research: A contextualist paradigm for rhetoric and composition. Logan, UT: Utah State University Press

Kanno, Y., & Harklau, L. (Eds.). (2012). *Linguistic minority students go to college: Preparation, access, and persistence.* New York, NY: Routledge.

Matsuda, P. K. (2003). Coming to voice: Publishing as a graduate student. In C. P. Casanave & S. Vandrick (Eds.), *Writing for scholarly publication: Behind the scenes in language education* (pp. 47–62). Mahwah, NJ: Lawrence Erlbaum Associates.

Matsuda, P. K. (1998). Situating ESL writing in a cross-disciplinary context. *Written Communication, 15*(1), 99–121.

Silva, T., & Leki, I. (2004). Family matters: The influence of applied linguistics and composition studies on second language writing studies—Past, present, and future. *The Modern Language Journal, 88*(1), 1–13.

# 7 Working Toward Being a Tenured Writing Program Administrator

*Tanita Saenkhum*

"Do not take or accept a WPA position until you get tenured," the renowned Duane Roen of Arizona State University (ASU), a former President of the Council of Writing Program Administrators, told us—my fellow graduate students and me—in his graduate seminar on writing program administration offered in 2007. To be honest, I did not really understand what Duane meant, so I did not take his caution seriously. But, now, I realize how challenging it is to take on administrative work while working toward tenure.

As this chapter is being written, I am in my third year as a pre-tenure writing program administrator (WPA) and concurrently am in my fourth year as a tenure-track assistant professor at my current institution, a research university. Drawing on my experience directing an ESL writing program as a pre-tenure WPA, I discuss challenges I have encountered, specifically focusing on expectations from my department and institution. I explore strategies I have developed in order to grapple with such challenges, particularly looking at how to make administrative work visible and valuable to colleagues. The goal is to illustrate how an individual navigates her professionalization process as well as to shed light on what it is like being an early-career L2 writing specialist at a U.S. institution of higher education.

## Personal and Institutional Context

Upon completion of my doctoral degree in English with a concentration in Rhetoric, Composition, and Linguistics from ASU in 2012, I started a tenure-track assistant professor position with a specialization in L2 writing in the Rhetoric, Writing, and Linguistics program in the Department of English at the University of Tennessee, Knoxville (UTK). I came to my institution knowing that administrative work was part of my job. However, I did not assume the Director of ESL position until my second year in 2013. With the administrative duty, my 2–2 teaching load was reduced to a 1–2 load. As a newcomer, I spent my first year adjusting myself to the department, institution, and town. I also took the first year to learn more about the ESL writing program, observing an English placement exam administration, participating in evaluating exam essays, and making placement recommendations for students (Saenkhum, 2014; Saenkhum, 2015). The process I went through is similar to what other pre-tenure WPAs encounter when starting their job (Adler-Kassner, 2008; Mueller, Dowell, Hunter, Pantelides, Kellejian, Garcia, Davies, & Frost, 2014).

To give the reader a sense of the program I am directing, I briefly present a snapshot of UTK's ESL Writing Program. For more than two decades, the program had been under the directorship of Ilona Leki, a renowned L2 writing specialist who retired in 2010. Currently, the program offers writing courses for L2 students, serving about 1,000 international students, both at the undergraduate and graduate levels. Countries represented include China, South Korea, Taiwan, Thailand, Saudi Arabia, Germany, and Brazil. In addition to the first-year L2 writing sequence, the program offers two academic writing courses, one for undergraduate students and the other for graduate students. There are about seven instructors teaching L2 writing courses, including four full-time lecturers (who have some TESOL and linguistics backgrounds). The rest of teachers are graduate teaching assistants (TAs), and most of them are trained in teaching L2 writing by taking an L2 writing practicum with me.

As the program director, my responsibilities include the following:

- Determine policies related to English course placement;
- Recruit, prepare, and supervise L2 writing instructors;
- Serve on a Composition Committee representing L2 writing concerns;

- Work with the Director of the First-Year Composition Program on matters related to L2 students;
- Work with faculty members in the English Department and other units (e.g., Undergraduate Program and Graduate Program) on issues related to L2 writing and L2 students;
- Serve as a liaison between the ESL Writing Program and other related stakeholders across campus, including faculty, academic advisors, the Admissions Offices (both graduate and undergraduate), the English Language Institute, the Center for International Education, and other units as needed.
- Lead faculty-development workshops within the English Department and across campus; and
- Serve as an advocate for L2 students.

In addition to my regular duties, I have worked on different tasks in order to better serve the needs of L2 writers at my institution. One of the major tasks was to create a separate academic writing course specifically designed for L2 graduate students. In the past, both L2 undergraduate and graduate students were placed into the same academic writing course. My rationale for this change is that the two groups of students have differing writing needs and language proficiency levels. The new course was approved and we started offering it in Fall 2015.

Looking at the list of my regular administrative duties and other related tasks, which I have performed for the past two years, I have come to realize why Duane suggested not accepting a WPA position to early career professionals. Can you imagine a newly-minted Ph.D. juggling research, teaching, and directing a writing program, not to mention advising and mentoring undergraduate and graduate students? Yet, the status quo of the WPA academic job market is quite opposite. Institutions are continuously hiring assistant professors to take on administrative responsibilities at the early stage of their career; this is evident from academic job advertisements.

## WPA Job Market

I share two recent academic job posts on an MLA job list in order to show the pre-tenure WPA job market that is ubiquitous and to illustrate responsibilities of tenure-track assistant professors with an administrative appointment.

The University of . . . is seeking applications for a tenure-track position as Assistant or Associate Professor of English, with specialization in L2 writing in English. The successful candidate will teach in areas such as language acquisition and other domains related to TESL. In addition, he or she will play a significant role in course and program development and administration. Position requires Ph.D. in Rhetoric/Composition with L2 writing specialization/concentration, Applied Linguistics, or related field, experience or strong interest in directing a writing program for multilingual students, a record of teaching excellence, and publications appropriate to the rank. Duties include active participation in graduate and undergraduate programs, both in the English department and in conjunction with relevant L2 faculty in other departments, plus significant research and publication . . .

The . . . University Department of English seeks a tenure-track Assistant or Advanced Assistant Professor in Rhetoric/Composition to serve as the Director of Composition starting Fall 2016. Qualifications: Applicants should have experience in administering a writing program along with research and teaching interests in writing program administration, faculty development, rhetorical theory, or composition theory. Experience working with multilingual writers, online writing courses, writing in the disciplines, and/or program assessment will be beneficial. Required: Ph.D. in rhetoric, composition, or related field; and Experience teaching college-level writing course. Responsibilities: The Director of Composition will oversee a required first-semester composition course along with a required junior-year composition course that emphasizes disciplinary awareness. Teaching load is 2:2; the incumbent receives a one course per year reduction for administrative work. Teaching opportunities may include undergraduate courses in composition, advanced composition, rhetoric, or upper-division nonfiction writing; as well as graduate courses in rhetoric, composition theory, and composition pedagogy . . .

I had to admit that when I was on the job market and saw advertisements of WPA-related jobs like these two, I was very excited and could not refrain from applying for those positions. I told myself: "It would be nice if I got to be a WPA." Those who currently are on the job market may feel the same as I used to. To help prepare those interested in a pre-tenure WPA position, I share some challenges I have faced and strategies I have developed.

## CHALLENGES FACED AND STRATEGIES DEVELOPED

Over the past two years, I have found being a WPA as a probationary assistant professor the most challenging. Writing program administration work, which is the university-wide service, takes considerable amount of time, energy, and effort. To illustrate what I have had to deal with, I discuss an important university-level task I have performed and other related responsibilities I have been requested to take on, and I describe the nature of WPA work that may put my tenure case at risk. A discussion of each challenge/issue is followed by strategies I have developed.

First, my institution, like other U.S. universities, has continuously recruited international students from all over the world. This recruitment has resulted in an influx of this diverse student population on campus in the past few years. As a response to this linguistic diversity, the Provost convened a Task Force on English Proficiency in Fall 2014 with the goal of developing a more streamlined and student-friendly approach to serving the needs of L2 students and to assisting them in becoming proficient in English language skills. I was appointed as one of the six members to the Provost's Task Force, and I was the only junior faculty serving on this group. At my university, in-house English placement exams had been the only means used to determine English course placement for L2 students. I proceeded to spearhead a new university-wide placement procedure of using standardized test scores (e.g., TOEFL, IELTS, SAT, and ACT) to guide placement of L2 students into writing courses; and if students are not satisfied with their placement based on test scores or do not have test scores, they may take an optional English placement exam. I am aware that standardized test scores may not tell how well students can write, as argued by L2 writing assessment scholars like Deborah Crusan (2002) who suggest a combination of measurements for placement. However, since our campus admits about 250–300 incoming international students each fall semester (about 75–100 students in spring), grading exam essays became impossible in a constrained period of time, specifically when we did not have enough qualified raters.

The new placement procedure program was piloted in Spring 2015, and this pilot program was based on data collection of previous students' standardized test scores and their course placement based on an in-house English placement exam. The data I collected demonstrated that undergraduate students with high TOEFL test scores (e.g., 90 out of 120 iBT) scored well in the English placement exam and were subsequently placed into a regular first-year writing course. For those with lower test scores, they did not do well in the placement exam and were placed into a developmental writing course (It is called Academic English for Undergraduate Students at our institution). The new placement procedure was put in place at the beginning of Fall 2015. It turned out that only 59 students (out of about 250 students) chose to take the optional English placement exam while the rest were satisfied with their placement based on standardized test scores.

While I worked on this important task, I also corresponded and met with related academic units, including the undergraduate and graduate admissions offices, the international students office, and academic advisors, informing them how the new procedure worked and what kind of help and cooperation we needed from them. While the administrative task was finished, I was not able to complete my research as planned, especially making little progress in my writing in that semester.

*Strategy: Through Documentation.* I document what I do as the Director of ESL and share it with colleagues, especially in retention meetings, through my department head and faculty mentor. At UTK, every new tenure-track assistant professor is assigned to a faculty mentor who is a tenured professor in the same department. The faculty mentor may or may not come from the same field. My mentor specializes in Renaissance literature and culture.

Since I started taking over the director of ESL position, I have documented everything related to my administrative work. This kind of evidence speaks for itself and makes everyone in the department understand what I have had to deal with as I work toward my tenure as a tenure-track assistant professor who takes on administrative duties at the same time. As a result of this documentation, my 1–2 teaching load was reduced to a 1–1 load in the academic year of 2015–2016. This course release was to compensate for the additional administrative responsibilities handed to me over the last few academic years. I am fortunate that my department head, faculty mentor, and colleagues understand my situation, and they are trying their best to provide support. I remember hearing tenured professors telling us tenure-track assistant professors: "We want you to do well, and we want to see you succeed."

Second, I am the only L2 writing specialist who is professorial faculty on campus, and this means I have always been invited to serve on various L2-and applied linguistics-related committees. For example, I was invited to join a committee initiated for international teaching assistants. I was invited to serve on a Spanish Applied Linguistics search committee for the Modern Foreign Languages and Literatures department. These requests mostly come from other units and departments. While I did not think I could take on these additional roles, I found it difficult to say no to those requests. Even now, I am still learning to say no more diplomatically. I believe what I have encountered here is similar to what other L2 writing specialists at other institutions have dealt with. Like Shuck (2006) puts it, "being 'the ESL person on campus' is, to say the least, an enormous responsibility" (p. 65). My collaborators and I (Saenkhum, Chamcharatsri, Kim, Iida, & Ruecker, 2014) argued in our colloquium on professional pathways of early-career L2 writing specialists at the 13th Symposium on Second Language Writing that "L2 writing specialists are often the lone L2 writing person in their new institutions, which means their services are requested by a variety of individuals and bodies."

*Strategy: Through Faculty Mentor and Department Head.* Since I did not know what to do and how to handle those requests, I then brought them to my faculty mentor and department head in order to seek for advice from them. Luckily, both of them have been aware of my administrative situation and recommended that I say no to those invitations. By consulting them, I was finally able to decline without feeling pressure or guilt. I also communicate with my faculty mentor and keep him informed about my research progress and other related concerns and issues. The more I communicate with him about my work, the more he will be able to understand what I do and what it means if I publish in Journal A or Journal B, and he will be able to speak on behalf of me, especially in retention meetings.

Third, the nature of the WPA work may put my tenure case at risk, especially when I am in a department where the majority of faculty members are literature professors. It is not unusual that people coming from different fields and disciplines tend to believe that WPA and L2 writing scholarship is not theory-based or grounded; it is rather "applied" in their view. I have experienced this myself. One of my colleagues asked whether my book manuscript on the placement of multilingual students into first-year composition courses (Saenkhum, 2016) would be more applied rather than theoretical because of the nature of the field of rhetoric and composition. My situation echoes what former WPA Jeanne Gunner (2002) reveals: "Helping colleagues to understand WPA as an academic and scholarly endeavor has been and is a difficult task, and it is likely to continue for some time to be the pivotal issue in WPA tenure cases" (p. 315).

*Strategy: Through Research.* The most important question is: What are some ways to make colleagues in a traditional English department understand the nature of my WPA and L2 writing work? In other words, how to make them realize that what I do is "scholarship." It is not just a "service" as they may understand. With this in mind, I use the writing program as a site of my research (Donahue, 2016; Rose & Weiser, 1999). Most of my research projects are based on what I do as a WPA, including placement, curriculum design and development, writing teacher preparation and development, and students' success and failure in writing courses. This is to show my colleagues that I am establishing myself as an individual scholar based on my specialization. For example, in my recent retention narrative, which was read by tenured faculty, I wrote:

> Over the past five years, I have been examining the placement of multilingual students in U.S. college composition programs in order to generate a better understanding of and to improve the placement practices for this student population. One of my main arguments is that students' perspectives should be included in the overall programmatic placement decisions.

Additionally, I seek moral support and help from fellow assistant professors who are in the same situation—working toward tenure (Saenkhum, 2015). We create our own academic network in which members of our group are encouraged to share and discuss academic-related issues and other personal stories and experiences. My fellow assistant professors (see Chamcharatsri, Kim, Iida, and Ruecker in this volume) are folks I knew since we were graduate students. We met at conferences, became friends, and collaborated in conference presentations and research projects.

## Final Thoughts

It has become common that junior faculty members, especially tenure-track assistant professors, are asked to take on administrative responsibilities in their early career; therefore, it is fundamental that institutions and departments develop an understanding of challenges that young scholars encounter while working toward their tenure. For tenure-track assistant professors with an administrative appointment, it is crucial that we continue communicating and informing colleagues about what (research) we do and what our administration work entails. Communication matters.

## References

Adler-Kassner, L. (2008). *The activist WPA: Changing stories about writing and writers.* Logan, UT: Utah State University Press.

Crusan, D. (2002). An assessment of ESL writing placement assessment. *Assessing Writing, 8*(1) 17–30.

Donahue, C. (2016). What is WPA research? In R. Malenczyk (Ed.), *A rhetoric for writing program administrators* (pp. 446–459). Anderson, SC: Parlor Press.

Gunner, J. (2002). Professional advancement of the WPA: Rhetoric and politics in tenure and promotion." In I. Ward & W. J. Carpenter (Eds.), *The Allyn & Bacon sourcebook for writing program administrators* (pp. 315–330). New York, NY: Longman.

Mueller, D., Dowell, M., Hunter, R., Pantelides, K., Kellejian, K., Garcia, M., Davies, L., & Frost, A. (2014, March). *Polymorphic frames of pre-tenure WPAs: Eight accounts of hybridity and pronoia.* Paper presented at Conference on College Composition and Communication, Indianapolis, Indiana.

Rose, S. & Weiser, I. (Eds.). *The writing program administrator as researcher: Inquiry in action and reflection.* Portsmouth, NH: Heinemann-Boyton/Cook.

Saenkhum, T. (2014, March). *Exploring ways to balance research, administrative work, and teaching as a pre-tenure writing program administrator.* Paper presented at TESOL International Convention and English Language Expo, Portland, Oregon.

Saenkhum, T. (2015). Choices in identity building as an L2 writing specialist: Investment and perseverance. In K. McIntosh, C. Pelaez-Morales, & T. Silva (Eds.), *Graduate studies in second language writing* (pp. 111–125). Anderson, SC: Parlor Press.

Saenkhum, T. (2016). Decisions, agency, and advising: Key issues in the placement of multilingual writers into first-year composition courses. Logan, UT: Utah State University Press.

Saenkhum, T., Chamcharatsri, P. B., Kim, S. H., Iida, A., & Ruecker, T. (2014, November). *Exploring the professional pathways of early-career L2 writing specialists*. Paper presented at Symposium on Second Language Writing, Tempe, Arizona.

Shuck, G. (2006). Combating monolingualism: A novice administrator's Challenge. *WPA: Writing Program Administration, 30* (1/2): 59–82.

# 8 Fake It 'Til You Make It: The Imposter Phenomenon in Gendered Academia

*Deborah Crusan*

### INTRODUCTION

The Imposter Phenomenon, sometimes called Imposter Syndrome or Fraud Syndrome, is a psychological phenomenon in which people are unable to internalize their accomplishments. Despite external evidence of their competence, those with the syndrome remain convinced that they are frauds and do not deserve the success they have achieved. Proof of success is dismissed as luck, timing, or as a result of deceiving others into thinking they are more intelligent and competent than they believe themselves to be (Clance, 1985b; Clance & Imes, 1975; Kay & Shipman, 2014; Young, 2011). Symptoms of the Imposter Phenomenon include self-doubt, a sense of incompetence, fear, immobility, and stress. Factors such as societal perceptions, race, culture, family, class, gender, age, and sexual orientation may exacerbate these feelings of inadequacy.

In her autobiography (1977/2010), Agatha Christie confessed that she often felt as though she was pretending to be something she was not—she was pretending to be a *successful author*. Anyone reading these words might feel a niggle of doubt, wondering how someone as famous and venerated as Agatha Christie could question her own vast accomplishments, and that she could possibly suffer from the Imposter Phenomenon. There are other sufferers, many of them prominent celebrities with enviable lists of roles, publications, awards, and street credibility.

Young (2011) chronicles several well-known public figures including Academy Award winner Meryl Streep, who has wrestled with the phenomenon. Streep remarked, "You think, 'Why would anyone want to see me again in a movie? And I don't know how to act, so why am I doing this?'" She is not alone. Kate Winslet once commented, "[I would] wake up in the morning before going to a shoot and think, 'I can't do this; I'm a fraud.'" The late author Maya Angelou declared, "I have eleven books, but each time I think, 'Uh-oh, they're going to find out now. I've run a game on everybody, and they're going to find me out.'" Former CEO of Girls, Inc, Joyce Roche stated that "somewhere deep inside, you don't believe what they say. You think it's a matter of time before you stumble and 'they' discover the truth."

Even Christine Lagarde, Eleventh Managing Director of the International Monetary Fund, has confessed to imposter feelings. She remarked, "We assume, somehow, that we don't have the level of expertise to be able to grasp the whole thing." She over prepares for every task, large or small, and commiserates with the Chancellor of Germany, Angela Merkel, a fellow sufferer. Neil Gaiman, whose books and stories have been honored with countless prizes internationally, including the Newbery and Carnegie Medals, admits to having battles with the fraud police.

Finally, in her all-important book *Lean In,* Sheryl Sandberg (2013), Chief Operating Officer of Facebook confesses to imposter feelings in her years at Harvard and in her early career. These men and women are not alone; thousands of high-achieving professionals report experiencing burgeoning doubt that they have somehow fooled their way to the top and any day they will be discovered for the charlatans they are.

## The Imposter Phenomenon

Clance and Imes (1978) first coined the term Imposter Phenomenon. They observed that some high-achieving individuals secretly believe that they cannot live up to others' expectations. They deeply personalize failures and mistakes and may convince themselves that their success is based on luck or timing, not on their own experience, skills, or other qualities. In many cases, imposter feelings can often be traced to early family or school dynamics if a child received mixed messages concerning competency and individual achievements. According to Clance and Imes (1978), imposter phenomenon is most likely to occur in those for whom success came quickly, first-generation professionals, people with high-achieving parents, members of minority groups, and students.

Dancy and Brown (2011) provide the following subcategories of imposter phenomenon:

- *feeling like a fake,* or the belief that one does not deserve his or her success or professional position and that somehow others have been deceived into thinking otherwise;
- *attributing success to luck,* that is, to external reasons rather than to one's own internal abilities; and
- *discounting success,* or the tendency to downplay or disregard academic or personal achievement. These categories especially in relationship to gender are woven through the remainder of the chapter.

## THE IMPOSTER PHENOMENON IN ACADEMIA

As Applied Linguistics/Second Language Writing scholars, it is important to understand how Imposter feelings might affect the work we do as writing scholars, as teachers, as conference presenters, and as mentors of the next generation of scholars, particularly if we suffer from the innate fear of being unmasked as something we are not (Brookfield, 1995). That is, we can neither tailor nor expand professional development opportunities for our mentees if we cannot envision ourselves as worthy to approach our colleagues or qualified to mentor others.

Regarding faculty struggles with imposter phenomenon, Hutchins (2015) reports moderately high prevalence for feelings of fraud in her survey of faculty at four-year institutions. Besides producing evidence that academic faculty indeed experience imposter thoughts, she documented and reported that such experiences are more prevalent for untenured faculty. Further, she found that "imposter tendencies were positively and significantly related to emotional exhaustion" (p. 8) and that faculty use adaptive coping skills to suppress imposter thoughts. Her results highlight the multidimensional role that mentors play as both supporters aiding in the reversal of the tendency for faculty to attribute their success to factors outside themselves and also as challengers helping to shape the faculty member's identity development by influencing their attributional process.

In their discussion of teachers of color and their mentorship into the academy, Dancy and Brown (2011) focus on the Imposter Phenomenon as an "internalized, reproducing, negative influence in the professional lives of scholars of color and the future education leaders they prepare" (p. 615). They report that teachers of color wrestle with conflicting feelings about their development as scholars. The authors recount conversations in educational leadership professional development programs in which students of color describe their struggles to find support and mentorship in their research, particularly if they wish to study topics of interest to marginalized communities since many faculty share neither their interest nor experience.

## Gender and Confidence

Chimamanda Ngozi Adichie in her TED Talk *We Should All Be Feminists* remarks: "We teach girls to shrink themselves, to make themselves smaller. We say to girls, 'You can have ambition, but not too much. You should aim to be successful, but not too successful, otherwise you would threaten the man.'" All this is true. Women are much more likely to feel this way, because women are taught to be modest and self-deprecating, to downplay their achievements for fear of looking arrogant or ungrateful. Often, high standards for expecting perfection compound those feelings, especially when falling short of expectations. And even though Clance and Imes found no evidence in 1978, there is anecdotal evidence that women are often more affected than men by the Imposter Phenomenon (Kay & Shipman, 2014; Young, 2011).

As a general rule, women tend to refer to their accomplishments less frequently than men do. One recent large cross-disciplinary study finds that these patterns extend to self-citation, documenting the self-citation habits of men and women in academe. King, Correll, Jacquet, Bergstrom, and West (2015) claim that citation counts—and they found that men do indeed practice self-citation much more regularly than women—can affect careers, both directly and indirectly. They add:

> Given the importance of metrics of scholarly influence in academic hiring, tenure and salary decisions, examining gender

differences in citation patterns may shed light on persisting gender discrepancies in faculty hiring and promotion. More broadly, academic publishing provides an illustrative case for gender differences in evaluation metrics and workplace advancement. (p. 1)

Along with this propensity for men to self-cite more than women is the tendency to externalize rather than internalize. Dr. Sheila Widnall, professor of aeronautics and astronautics at Massachusetts Institute of Technology and former secretary of the U.S. Air Force is credited with saying, "Treat a male student badly and he will think you're a jerk. Treat a female student badly and she will think you have finally discovered that she doesn't belong in engineering."

As mentioned earlier, part of the reason that women tend to feel fraudulent stems from socialization patterns. It seems that girls are socialized to be concerned with fairness, openness, and politeness. Of girls, Young (2011) remarks, "If you do something wrong, you apologize" (p. 213). She notes the gender difference when she claims, "Boys on the other hand learn that saying I'm sorry is a sign of weakness" (Young, 2011, p. 213).

Along with the politeness factor is the confidence factor. Confidence, how to get it, who has it, who does not have it, and why has received quite a bit of attention. Babcock, Gelfand, Small, and Stayn (2006) examined confidence levels in men and women regarding salary negotiation; their study reveals that men initiate salary negotiations four times as often as women, and when women do negotiate, they ask for 30 percent less than men do. In terms of how much they will initially earn, men reveal that they expect to earn significantly more ($80,000) than women expect ($64,000). In general these scholars believe that women lack the confidence that men have.

Kay and Shipman (2014) define confidence as "the purity of action produced by a mind free of doubt" (p. 3). They conducted interviews about confidence and found that women often doubt their abilities, thinking they can never be good enough. In their interview with Mike Thibault, head coach of the Women's National Basketball Association (WNBA) Washington Mystics, Thibault discussed his experiences training both male and female athletes. He believes that the propensity to dwell on failure and mistakes and an inability to shut out the outside world are the biggest psychological impediments in his female players. He noted that the best male players are equally hard on themselves, but they do not let setbacks linger as long. Several of his female players agreed that it is hard for them to let go of past failures.

Clearly, confidence, or rather the lack of confidence, weighs heavily in the Imposter Phenomenon. Kay and Shipman (2014) interviewed Brenda Major, a social psychologist at the University of California Santa Barbara. Major sets up protocols in which she asks men and women to estimate their performance on a variety of tests. She found that "men consistently overestimate their abilities and subsequent performance and women routinely underestimate both" (p. 16).

These scholars, as a group, agree that having confidence skewed to the positive is a good thing. Kay and Shipman (2014) add, "Men worry less about upsetting their superiors because unlike their sisters, they haven't been trained to fall into line, and their brains aren't wired to be as sensitive to criticism" (p. 174), which might explain boys' general ability to shrug off nagging parents, break curfews, and refuse to take showers. Men generally think they are pretty awesome, but as a rule, they do not appear arrogant because they genuinely believe that they are competent and smart. As a group, women need to start believing the same things about themselves (Adichie, 2013; Clance & Imes, 1978; Kay & Shipman, 2014; Young, 2011).

## Present Study

In an effort to explore the effect of the Imposter Phenomenon on academics, I conducted a study, which included an online survey and follow up interviews. Participants for this study completed Clance's (1985a) Imposter Phenomenon Quiz (see Appendix), which was posted online using Qualtrics software. Participants were recruited through an email sent through various Internet listservs (e.g., Language Testing Research and Practice, Second Language Writing Standing Group at the Conference on College Composition and Communication, Second Language Writing Interest Section at TESOL). The participants in this study (n = 217) were largely professionals in the fields of Applied Linguistics, TESOL Education, Language Testing, Composition and Rhetoric, Creative Writing, Teacher Education, Sociology, Social Work, History, and Educational Psychology and ranged in age from 22 to 73 with a median age of 41.

Cronbach's alpha for the survey was .947 meaning that the survey was extremely reliable. In this sample, *sex,* whether the participant was a male or a female, was highly significant as a predictor variable for the Imposter Phenomenon ($p < .001$); in other words, for the population in this data set, a woman is more likely to suffer from the Imposter Phenomenon than a man. The other highly significant predictor variable is age ($p < .004$.), so in this sample, the younger the respondent, the more likely he or she is to suffer from the Imposter Phenomenon. Finally, in *this* study, race, education, and field were not significant variables.

In regard to the responses to the Imposter Phenomenon Quiz, the mean was 61 with a standard deviation of 16.95. As can be seen in Table 1 below, on Clance's scale, this score of 61 indicates that the population documented in this study is on the lower end of frequent imposter feelings. Also note that the higher the score, the more frequently and seriously the Imposter Phenomenon interferes in a person's life.

Table 1. Clance (1985a) Scale

| SCORE | INTERPRETATION |
| --- | --- |
| 40 or less | Few Imposter characteristics |
| 41–60 | Moderate IP experiences |
| 61–80 | Frequent Imposter feelings |
| Higher than 80 | Often intense IP experiences |

A closer look at several of the survey questions reveals the breadth of the Imposter Phenomenon in this population. Question 13 on the survey reads: *Sometimes I'm afraid others will discover how much knowledge or ability I really lack.* The survey asked participants to choose one of five answers: Not true at all, Rarely, Sometimes, Often, or Very true. Of the 211 respondents who answered this question, 39 (18%) answered Often and 35 (17%) answered Very true for a combined total of 74 (35%) of respondents who worry about their perceived lack of knowledge or ability.

Another question that produced particularly interesting results is Question 5: *I sometimes think I obtained my present position or gained my present success because I happened to be in the right place at the right time or knew the right people.* This question was answered by 215 respondents. Forty-two (20%) answered Often and 42 (20%) answered

Very true for a combined total of 84 (40%) of respondents who believe persons or events outside themselves are responsible for their success.

In order to explore gender and confidence in more depth, data were gathered using face-to-face interviews conducted with faculty members at a mid-size Midwestern university; data reported in this study is from four women faculty who use the pseudonyms Gabriella, Salma, Louise, and Elizabeth. These data are summarized and in the form of actual quotes. These quotes focus on the topics of gender, feeling like a fake, discounting success, and attributing success to luck.

A particularly telling remark from the interview data drives the gender difference argument home. Gabriella, a young and quite successful Associate Professor of Renaissance Drama and Early Modern Culture has won grants and fellowships from places like the National Endowment of the Humanities Summer Institute and has publications in the top literature, culture, and women's studies journals internationally. She remarks about her place as a minority woman in her field. "I am a woman and a person of color in a very male-dominated, established, canonical field, so most of the people around me will be older white men; I have had, especially as a graduate student, many experiences of feeling resistance [to my gender and race] right off the bat."

Needing to compete with men and not feeling confident in their ability to do so was brought up again and again in the interviews. Even Salma, professor of history and author of three important books, who scored quite low (36 out of a possible 100) on the Clance Imposter Phenomenon Quiz (1985a) remarked in her interview response how she might be compared to men: "I was in history—a male dominated world, and I was 18 or 19, and I was forced to now be surrounded by men after living in a safe environment all through high school—an all girls school for 7 years—that I would now be underestimated."

A fascinating example of attributing one's success to luck is Louise, the author of two very successful short story collections; additionally, her stories have appeared in *Prairie Schooner* and other prestigious literary magazines. She has had fellowships to The Sewanee Writers' Conference and the Middlebury Bread Loaf Writers' Conference among others. She remarked, "I look back and I was publishing a lot and things were going my way, but it was always with the sense—it was kind of a fluke."

From Louise's words, it is evident that the Imposter Phenomenon tends to affect people who believe that their success was somehow an accident; it equally affects those who do not value themselves or their skills enough and who focus on their shortcomings instead of their good qualities. An example of this is Elizabeth, a full professor of social work, chair of her department, and former director of the Center for Teaching and Learning at her university. She has publications in top social work journals, but she clearly demonstrates a penchant for devaluing her own skills when she remarks, "It was always these other people who got PhDs and had some magical power or a super hero cape or way bigger brain than mine."

Finally, creative writer Louise described how she discounted success when she disclosed, "But I convinced myself if I could do it, it must not have been that hard. Like when I got a PhD—well clearly that's not as big of a deal as I thought. Publishing a book—well it must not be as hard as everyone thought it was. I got an agent—oh well, that must not be that big of a deal. So it's not that I think I don't deserve it; it's that I think it must not be that hard to get, all evidence to the contrary."

## My Story

Urged on by its power, I use narrative in this chapter to tell my story. Casanave (2010) reminds us that "narrative can help bring diverse perspectives into awareness and focus, and thus enable them to contribute to change and growth in our work and professional lives" (p. 8). She adds, "Without the telling, the many perspectives on ourselves and on the selves of others remain unarticulated, and hence invisible for reflection, scrutiny, or analysis over time" (p. 8). Through the following narrative, it is plain to see that I embody each of the categories represented in this chapter and in the literature on the Imposter Phenomenon: gender, feeling like a fake, discounting success, and attributing success to luck. I have always felt the tug of not being good enough. Especially in academic situations, whether it is publication or presentation, I believe that someone smarter, someone more accomplished, someone with more publications in better journals with higher impact factors, maybe somebody with more books, *somebody just better* is supposed to be doing what I am doing. And if I happen to mention these feelings of inadequacy, I am always amazed at the number of people who confess that they similarly experience these feelings. According to Clance and Imes (1978), Young (2011), and Kay and Shipman (2014), every high achieving person at one time or another has wrestled with the Imposter Phenomenon. These feelings are very real to the people who experience them, but some cannot understand them; so it appears (at least to me) that those who do not suffer might find it a bit difficult to understand why those of us who do just cannot simply *get over it*.

My struggle with the Imposter Phenomenon began very early. As in any study, there are certainly multiple variables at play that bear some responsibility for my imposter feelings and the 91 that I scored on Clance's survey. These include:

- I was born and raised in the era of children should be seen and not heard. I was taught NEVER to question authority; adults around me told me, "Do what I say, not what I do." As I was the first child, I did what I was told.
- I was *always* the good girl, never overstepping the boundaries set for me, never talking back, never demanding, never questioning. As a side note, Kay and Shipman (2014) discuss raising daughters and what to say and not to say to them. They contend that parents "subconsciously train our daughters not to speak up and demand to be heard, or demand most anything. The constant cycle of pressure and reward for good behavior doesn't help girls feel confident later in the rough-and-tumble world of the workplace" (p. 174).
- In general, my teachers did not provide an unbiased view of my intellect or capabilities; one teacher's cruel comments particularly stuck with me and molded the way I thought of myself from the 5th grade on.
- I did not do very well in high school. I credit this in part to the opinion of that one grade school teacher and its effect on my self-esteem.
- I left college after my sophomore year because I was not doing well and thought I was stupid.
- I married at 20 and married a misogynist, which served to cement my already festering low self-esteem.

Not until I returned to college in 1986 to finish a BS in English Education did I catch a glimpse of any intellect. I earned a 4.0 and graduated summa cum laude, but I discounted it, thinking it was nothing or that everyone earned the same honor. As has been previously stated, disregarding achievements and reduction of importance are trademarks of the Imposter Phenomenon, and I discount my successes very well. A few examples are:

- When I was accepted into graduate school at a very reputable university and was awarded a Teaching Assistantship, I supposed that there must not have been a very strong pool of applicants that year.
- When I finished both an MA and a PhD in five years, I thought that was what everybody did.
- When I got my job, I was convinced that the other two candidates must have been offered the job first and turned it down.
- When my first big publication was accepted, I was convinced that the editor was desperate for articles.
- When I was approached to write a book, I assumed bigger names had turned down the series editors.

I still struggle with this every day, and at times, I am frozen in my tracks, which is another hallmark of the imposter phenomenon—procrastination. Surprisingly, the above list of discounts is not all that uncommon. I am certainly not alone. Gabriella, one of the study interview participants, concurs: "When I got my first job offer, I thought, 'Well maybe the field wasn't so competitive that year, right, or maybe I wasn't the first ranked.'"

I have one other struggle. Although I am often perceived as gregarious and (mostly) self-assured, I struggle to maintain a confident facade *especially when making conference presentations*. However, I face two persistent problems: I look somewhat confident, and I look older; therefore, (I think) onlookers believe that I should know what I am doing and that I should be comfortable doing it since (I think they think) I surely have been doing it for a long time. I also think that they think I should have done more by now—more articles, more books, more plenaries, just more (Crusan, 2014).

## Coping Mechanisms

Young (2011) maintains that we do not choose to feel like imposters, but those who experience imposter feelings generally turn to four coping and protecting mechanisms. The first coping mechanism is diligence and hard work. If a person believes that everyone around him/her is inherently more intelligent or capable, one way to avoid detection is through extraordinary effort to the point of obsession to cover up supposed ineptness.

The next coping mechanism is holding back. When a person holds back, it is with the idea that if failure is certain, it is better that people think that laziness rather than stupidity was the cause. Holding back can also manifest through removing oneself from the possibility of promotion or avoiding anything that might expose vulnerability.

A third coping mechanism is charm. Using charm, one tries to find the right person to recognize his/her brilliance and help them embrace it. Sufferers use their social skills to impress this right person in the hopes that he/she will see them as intellectually special. The problem: if these efforts are successful, the charmer will then likely dismiss the positive feedback (Clance & Imes, 1978).

The final coping mechanism is procrastination. Procrastination is a way to put off any fear-inducing situation that might lead to eventual undoing. Everyone practices procrastination at times (e.g. cleaning everything in sight before tackling that revise and resubmit), but procrastination can provide a built in excuse for failure. The procrastinator might think: *I'm really disappointed that I didn't get the grant, but I'm not surprised—I whipped off the proposal at the last minute.*

## COMPETENCE

Those who suffer from the Imposter Phenomenon have a warped view of competence; this skewed reality is a major contributor to perpetuating the belief that one is an imposter. Where others see a highly competent person, the self-proclaimed phony sees an inadequate fraud—a view that bears little resemblance to reality. We make up competence rules, which include lots of bossy modals—*should* and *must*—and even bossier adverbs like *never* and *always*. We say things like *If I were really smart, I would always know what to say* or *Never raise your hand unless you are 100 percent sure you are right* or *Don't ask for help* or *Always over prepare.*

Young (2011) says: "Every imposter on the planet has a distorted view of competence. However, not all imposters skew it in the same way" (p. 106). She characterizes five competence types and then offers a substitution for old, unreasonable rules in what she calls the *Competence Rule Book for Mere Mortals*. Most people will recognize parts of themselves in several competence types although typically one type is dominant.

The first competence type is the perfectionist who views competence in this way: *I should deliver an unblemished performance 100% of the time. Every aspect of my work must be exemplary, Nothing short of perfection is acceptable.* Leonardo da Vinci has been credited with saying, "I have offended God and mankind because my work didn't reach the quality it should have." Da Vinci was one of the perfectionists who hold only themselves accountable, believing that if something needs to be done right, he must do it himself. Others impose their exacting standards on those around them. According to Young, some new competence rules for perfectionists are:

- Perfectionism inhibits success;
- Sometimes good is good enough; and
- Not everything deserves 100 percent.

The next competence type is the natural genius, who expects to know without being taught, to excel without effort, and to get it right on the first attempt. The natural genius thinks, *If I were a real writer, it wouldn't be this hard.* In fact, Michelangelo is credited with saying, "If people knew how hard I worked to get my mastery, it wouldn't seem so wonderful after all." Young recommends these new competence rules for natural geniuses:

- Effort trumps ability; and
- Real success takes time.

The expert is next; the expert's primary concern is how much knowledge or skill he/she possesses, and as far as the expert is concerned, there is never enough. The expert says *If I were really competent, I would know everything there is to know* or *Before I can put myself out there, I need in-depth education, training, and experience.* Women are especially prone to the expert trap, some astonishingly so. Unfortunately, Young (2011) reminds us that the cultural bias against female competence is well documented, so this might be a contributor. New competence rules for the expert are:

- There is no end to knowledge;
- Competence means respecting your limitations; and
- You do not need to know everything; you just need to be smart enough to find someone who does.

The fourth competence type is the rugged individualist. Rugged individualists spend years laboring under the misguided notion that true competence equals solo, unaided achievement. They fly solo because they believe that no one should need help. They say things like *If I were really competent, I could do everything myself.* They believe that the only true achievements are those accomplished entirely on their own. New competence rules for the rugged individualist are:

- Know how to ask for what you need and seek out people who know more than you do;
- Your work does not have to be groundbreaking to be good; and
- It's okay to build on the work of other competent people.

The final competence type is the Superwoman/SuperMan/SuperStudent whose competence rests on the ability to juggle multiple roles masterfully. Young (2011) claims that this is largely a cultural creation, which came into being when traditional roles of mother and homemaker were extended to accommodate the additional role of full-time paid worker. All of sudden, women, believed they needed to be all things to all people. Young likens this to "the perfectionist, the natural genius, and the rugged individualist on steroids" (p. 129). New competence rules for the Superwoman/man/student are:

- It's okay to say no;
- Delegate;
- Eliminating unnecessary tasks allows a focus on activities that really matter; and
- Being a Superperson sends an unhealthy message to our daughters and sons.

Young (2011) contends that there is a solution to extreme and unrealistic notions of what it takes to be competent. She recommends lowering the internal bar and adopting the *Competence Rule Book for Mere Mortals*.

## STRATEGIES

Along with the new competence rules Young recommends, there are numerous other strategies for managing the Imposter Phenomenon and gaining more confidence. One of the first strategies is to build confidence through a tactic that Kay and Shipman (2014) call bite-size failing, in which the person is instructed to complete one task at a time and to do it over and over until success is achieved. These tasks can include sending out a paper, applying for a grant, applying for a Fulbright. Bite-size failing teaches that there is no need to get everything right and that everyone fails some of the time.

Other strategies for building confidence include leaving the comfort zone and immediately acting on something without holding back, rewiring the brain to break the negative feedback loop by going through a list of achievements and successes, killing negative automatic thoughts by first recognizing them and writing them down for a few days then reframing the problem using a positive spin on the negative feeling (Sherman, 2013). *I'm not very efficient* can become *I'm doing a pretty good job of balancing so much.*

Support groups offer another coping strategy. When faced with the possibility of suffering with anything, be it psychological or physical, one can always find a support group, a collection of people who have experienced the same trauma that we have experienced. Whether these groups are led by a peer or a mental health professional, they generally have one goal in mind: to support others in similar situations. Groups meet face-to-face most often, but the growth of online support groups offer ways to connect as well. Further, groups offer coping strategies for a huge variety of conditions and issues such as acne, bulimia, alcohol abuse, adoption, bipolar disorder, various types of cancers, drug abuse (from A-Z), sex, gambling, insomnia, internet addiction, learning disabilities, miscarriage, obesity, online dating, and PTSD to catalog just a few of the more than 200 listed on just one website (http://online.supportgroups.com/). The point: people search for others who feel the same way or are experiencing difficulties with something; they look for strategies and support systems to overcome whatever situation they find themselves in.

This support system strategy has helped me tremendously. Because I am a social person, I focus on a project better when I am in a room with others. Back in 2008, I attended a weeklong writing boot camp at my university. It changed my world. While I understand that this kind of writing environment is not for everyone, it works for me. From that first and subsequent boot camps, a tight-knit group of seven women formed and through that group, we found that women thrive on WE; that is, women value camaraderie, enjoy celebrating each other's victories, and support and advance each other. In other words, women often succeed collectively.

The group initiated a monthly meeting at which we set goals, celebrate goals accomplished, and award silly prizes for achieved goals. This group of women has my back and will help me through any crisis, academic or personal. I know that they will read proposals, give advice, offer suggestions. It is comforting to know that as I navigate the politics of the university, I have these women to count on. We continue to write together, sending emails to schedule writing sessions. We have banded together to support each other through tenure and promotion by writing on weekdays and weekends if necessary. If someone has a deadline, as many of us as possible heed her call for writing support. We are also fighting to change the culture in which women are awarded tenure and subsequently are assigned heavy administrative duties that thwart chances for more research, writing, and publication.

Young (2011) recommends a strategy in which she asks clients to stop denying the evidence of their capabilities. She instead encourages clients to create an achievement history. She instructs, "Spill the beans about everything you've ever done—any shred of proof that you are, in fact, an intelligent, talented, resourceful, and otherwise fully capable human being" (p. 93). Young warns of the urge to explain away or underestimate accomplishments and reminds that we either got the grade or we did not. Achievement histories can be written lists of accomplishments or pictures representing goal realizations. They can be digital or handwritten. The only rule: simply list everything that has been accomplished without judgment or minimization.

Another helpful strategy is networking. I have one special story about the value of networking, and it's about Paul Kei Matsuda. I first met Paul at the inaugural Symposium on Second Language Writing at Purdue in 1998 when we were both still doctoral students. Paul was already on his way to stardom, and I was not. In 1999, I graduated and took a job at Wright State University in Dayton, OH. The very next year, Paul took a job at Miami of Ohio; I was in my second year at Wright State, very green although already 50. I constantly talked about how much Paul was publishing and how I wished that I could talk to him about his work. Finally, after much cajoling, I got up the nerve to email Paul and ask him if I could come to Miami and take him to lunch. I was *scared to death* that day driving to Oxford, but when I got there, Paul was inviting and kind. He showed me his office, answered my endless questions, and paraded me around campus. We went to lunch and have been friends ever since. There is never a time that I have felt that I cannot email him with a question. I have looked to him for advice and counsel more times than I can count. So find yourself **A** Paul (not **The** Paul) who will entertain your endless questions. But remember that even if someone opens the door for you, you are the one who walks through and delivers the goods.

Compelled by Paul's generous mentorship, I have felt the need to develop an avenue for guidance and support of young Applied Linguistic/TESOL scholars. This has taken the shape of an event held each year at TESOL, an event called An Evening with Friends of Second Language Writing. Started in 2007, the gathering facilitates networking between young scholars and those already established in the field. New scholars might be shy about approaching established figures in a field; the event creates an opportunity for interaction, idea exchange, and relationship building in order to further the careers of those in second language writing. This annual gathering serves an important purpose as evidenced by the increasing number of people attending every year. I believe sincerely in mentorship, and I believe the event has been influential for both new and established teachers and scholars.

Gabriella, an interview participant, agrees about the importance of mentoring. She says, "I think the other side of that [imposter] question is how do you get over it? This is where mentorship comes in—looking out for the kinds of strategies that help graduate students get over the hump to help [new scholars] erase ancillary concerns that have nothing to do with the work, and mentor them; bring them to conferences; introduce them to people."

## Conclusion

Throughout this chapter, it has been one of my intents to lay bare my struggle with the Imposter Phenomenon in the hope that readers might find something that helps them to recognize it, contain it, and possibly defeat it. But here's the dirty little secret—the feelings may not quickly or completely vanish. Rather, their roar will diminish to a whisper when the following strategies are implemented:

- Talk about imposter feelings with others;
- Do not be afraid;
- Keep track of accomplishments;
- Get a support system;
- Make realistic assessments; and

- Understand that you know as much as anyone else.

The mantra *I will hold myself to a standard of grace, not perfection* is a powerful one. You *are* good enough.

## References

Babcock, L., Gelfand, M., Small, D. & Stayn, H. (2006). Gender differences in the propensity to initiate negotiations. In D. De Cremer, M. Zeelenberg, & J. K. Murnighan (Eds), *Social Psychology and Economics*, Lawrence Erlbaum, Mahwah, NJ, pp. 239–59.

Brookfield, S. (1995). *Becoming a critically reflective teacher.* San Francisco: Jossey-Bass.

Casanave, C. P. (2010). Perspective taking. In A. M. Stoke (Ed.), *JALT 2009 Conference Proceedings.* Tokyo: JALT.

Adichie, C. N. (2013, April 12). We should all be feminists [Video file]. Retrieved from https://www.youtube.com/watch?v=hg3umXU_qWc

Clance, P. R. (1985a). The Imposter Phenomenon: When Success Makes You Feel Like a Fake (pp. 20 -22). Toronto: Bantam Books.

Clance, P. R. (1985b). *The imposter phenomenon: Overcoming the fear that haunts your success.* Atlanta: Peachtree Publishers.

Clance, P. R., & Imes, S. (1978). The imposter phenomenon in high achieving women: Dynamics and therapeutic intervention. *Psychotherapy: Theory, Research, and Practice, 15* (3), 241–247.

Christie, A. (1977/2010). *An autobiography.* New York: Harper Collins.

Crusan, D. (2014, November). Fake it 'till you make it: The imposter syndrome—the dilemma of (women) academics. Plenary at the Symposium on Second Language Writing, Arizona State University, Tempe, AZ, November 15, 2014.

Dancy, II, T. E., & Brown, II, M. C. (2011). The mentoring and induction of educators of color: Addressing the imposter syndrome in academe. *Journal of School Leadership, 21,* 607-634.

Hutchins, H. L. (2015). Outing the imposter: A study exploring imposter phenomenon among higher education faculty. *New Horizons in Adult Education & Human Resource Development, 27*(2), 3–12.

Kay, K., & Shipman, C. (2014). *The confidence code: The science and art of self-assurance—what women should know.* New York: Harper Collins.

King, M. M., Correll, S. J., Jacquet, J., Bergstrom, C. T., & West, J. D. (2015). *Men set their own cites high: Gender and self-citation across fields and over time.* Unpublished manuscript.

Online support groups. (n. d.).Retrieved from http://online.supportgroups.com/

Sandberg, S. (2013). *Lean in: Women, work, and the will to lead.* New York, NY: Alfred A. Knopf.

Sherman, R.O. (2013). Imposter syndrome: When you feel like you're faking it. *American Nurse Today, 8*(5), 57–58.

Young, V. (2011). *The secret thoughts of successful women: Why capable people suffer from the impostor syndrome and how to thrive in spite of it.* New York: Crown Publishing.

## Appendix: Clance IP Scale

For the following questions, please give the first response that enters your mind rather than dwelling on each statement and thinking about it over and over.

1. I have often succeeded on a test or task even though I was afraid that I would not do well before I undertook the task.
1 (not at all true)   2 (rarely)   3 (sometimes)   4 (often)   5 (very true)

2. I can give the impression that I'm more competent than I really am.
1 (not at all true)   2 (rarely)   3 (sometimes)   4 (often)   5 very true)

3. I avoid evaluations if possible and have a dread of others evaluating me.
1 (not at all true)   2 (rarely)   3 (sometimes)   4 (often)   5 very true)

4. When people praise me for something I've accomplished, I'm afraid I won't be able to live up to their expectations of me in the future.
1 (not at all true)   2 (rarely)   3 (sometimes)   4 (often)   5 very true)

5. I sometimes think I obtained my present position or gained my present success because I happened to be in the right place at the right time or knew the right people.
1 (not at all true)   2 (rarely)   3 (sometimes)   4 (often)   5 (very true)

6. I'm afraid people important to me may find out that I'm not as capable as they think I am.
1 (not at all true)   2 (rarely)   3 (sometimes)   4 (often)   5 very true)

7. I tend to remember the incidents in which I have not done my best more than those times I have done my best.
1 (not at all true)   2 (rarely)   3 (sometimes)   4 (often)   5 very true)

8. I rarely do a project or task as well as I'd like to do it.
1 (not at all true)   2 (rarely)   3 (sometimes)   4 (often)   5 very true)

9. Sometimes I feel or believe that my success in my life or in my job has been the result of some kind of error.
1 (not at all true)   2 (rarely)   3 (sometimes)   4 (often)   5 very true)

10. It's hard for me to accept compliments or praise about my intelligence or accomplishments.
1 (not at all true)   2 (rarely)   3 (sometimes)   4 (often)   5 very true)

11. At times, I feel my success has been due to some kind of luck.
1 (not at all true)   2 (rarely)   3 (sometimes)   4 (often)   5 very true)

12. I'm disappointed at times in my present accomplishments and think I should have accomplished much more.
1 (not at all true)   2 (rarely)   3 (sometimes)   4 (often)   5 very true)

13. Sometimes I'm afraid others will discover how much knowledge or ability I really lack.
1 (not at all true)   2 (rarely)   3 (sometimes)   4 (often)   5 very true)

14. I'm often afraid that I may fail at a new assignment or undertaking even though I generally do well at what I attempt.
1 (not at all true)   2 (rarely)   3 (sometimes)   4 (often)   5 very true)

15. When I've succeeded at something and received recognition for my accomplishments, I have doubts that I can keep repeating that success.
1 (not at all true)   2 (rarely)   3 (sometimes)   4 (often)   5 (very true)

16. If I receive a great deal of praise and recognition for something I've accomplished, I tend to discount the importance of what I've done.
1 (not at all true)   2 (rarely)   3 (sometimes)   4 (often)   5 (very true)

17. I often compare my ability to those around me and think they may be more intelligent than I am.
1 (not at all true)   2 (rarely)   3 (sometimes)   4 (often)   5 (very true)

18. I often worry about not succeeding with a project or examination, even though others around me have considerable confidence that I will do well.
1 (not at all true)   2 (rarely)   3 (sometimes)   4 (often)   5 (very true)

19. If I'm going to receive a promotion or gain recognition of some kind, I hesitate to tell others until it is an accomplished fact.
1 (not at all true)   2 (rarely)   3 (sometimes)   4 (often)   5 (very true)

20. I feel bad and discouraged if I'm not "the best" or at least "very special" in situations that involve achievement.
1 (not at all true)   2 (rarely)   3 (sometimes)   4 (often)   5 (very true)

The above questionnaire is from *The Imposter Phenomenon: When Success Makes You Feel Like a Fake* (pp. 20 -22), by P. R. Clance, 1985, Toronto: Bantam Books. Copyright 1985 by Pauline Rose Clance, Ph.D., ABPP. Reprinted by permission. Bantam Books. The Imposter Test was developed to help individuals determine whether or not they have Imposter Phenomenon characteristics and, if so, to what extent they are suffering.

If the total score is 40 or less, the respondent has few Imposter characteristics; if the score is between 41 and 60, the respondent has moderate IP experiences; a score between 61 and 80 means that the respondent frequently has Imposter feeling; and a score higher than 80 means the respondent often has intense IP experiences. The higher the score, the more frequently and seriously the Imposter Phenomenon interferes in a person's life.

# Contributors

**Dwight Atkinson** is an applied linguist and second language educator currently teaching at the University of Arizona. His recent work includes a chapter on the place of "culture" in second language writing, appearing in the *Handbook of Second and Foreign Language Writing* (2017), and research on collaborative writing as a sociocognitive endeavor, co-authored with Takako Nishino, appearing in the *Journal of Second Language Writing* (2015).

**Pisarn Bee Chamcharatsri** is Assistant Professor with joint appointments in the Department of Language, Literacy and Sociocultural Studies and the Department of English Language and Literature at the University of New Mexico, where he teaches writing-related courses to undergraduate international students and courses in applied linguistics to graduate international students. His research interests include emotionality in language learning and teaching, second language writing, identity construction, SLA, and world Englishes. His publications appear in *L2 Journal, Journal of Writing Assessment, Asian EFL Journal*, and other edited collections. He received his PhD in Composition and TESOL from Indiana University of Pennsylvania.

**Deborah Crusan** is Professor of TESOL/Applied Linguistics at Wright State University, Dayton, OH. Her work has appeared in academic publications and edited collections about second language writing. Her research interests include writing assessment, writing teacher education, directed self-placement and its consequences for second language writers, and the politics of assessment. Her book, *Assessment in the Second Language Writing Classroom*, was published by University of Michigan Press. She and Todd Ruecker are finalizing *The Politics of English Second Language Writing Assessment in Global Contexts* for publication with Routledge. Currently, she serves on the TESOL International Association Board of Directors (2016-2019).

**Atsushi Iida** is Associate Professor of English in the University Education Center at Gunma University, Japan. He earned his Ph.D. in English (Composition and TESOL) at Indiana University of Pennsylvania. His research interests include second language writing, poetry writing, literature in second language education, and writing for academic publication. He has published his work in various journals including *Assessing Writing, System, Scientific Study of Literature, English Teaching Forum,* and *Asian EFL Journal*.

**Soo Hyon Kim** is Assistant Professor at the University of New Hampshire where she teaches courses in second language writing, second language acquisition, and TESOL. Her research focuses on second language writing, English for Academic Purposes, and research methods. Soo's current projects include examining the use of research methods within the field of second language writing, and exploring graduate writers' development of scholarly identities. She is also involved in several on-going collaborative projects on graduate writing support and writing across/in the disciplines, and has co-edited a special issue in *Across the Disciplines*: "Graduate Reading and Writing Across the Curriculum."

**Todd Ruecker** is Assistant Professor of English at the University of New Mexico. His research focuses on investigating issues surrounding the increasing linguistic and cultural diversity of education systems and making institutions and classrooms more welcoming spaces for all students. He has published articles in respected composition, education, and applied linguistics journals such as *TESOL Quarterly* and *College Composition and Communication*. He has published one monograph (*Transiciones: Pathways of Latinas and Latinos Writing in High School and College*) and has co-edited two collections (*Linguistically Diverse Immigrant and Resident Writers: Transitions from High School to College* and *Retention, Persistence, and Writing Programs*).

**Tanita Saenkhum** is Assistant Professor of English at the University of Tennessee, Knoxville, where she directs the ESL Writing Program and teaches courses in L2 writing, TESOL, and SLA. Her first book, *Decisions, Agency, and Advising: Key Issues in the Placement of Multilingual Writers into First-Year Composition Courses*, (Utah State University Press, 2016), considers the role of students' own agency in the placement of multilingual writers in US college composition programs. She has published in *Journal of Second Language Writing*,

*WPA: Writing Program Administration*, and *Journal of English for Academic Purposes*. Her scholarship has also appeared in several edited collections.

**Christine M. Tardy** is Professor of English Applied Linguistics at University of Arizona, where she teaches courses in applied linguistics/TESOL and writing studies. Her research explores second language writing, academic writing, genre theory and practice, and the policies and politics of English. Her work has been published in numerous journals and edited collections, including her recent book, *Beyond Convention: Genre Innovation in Academic Writing* (University of Michigan, 2016). She served as co-editor of *Journal of Second Language Writing* from 2011 to 2016.

# Index

Ablex Publishing Corporation, 10
academic advisor, 54, 62–63, 82, 85
academic journal, 24, 60, 62, 78
academic voice, 68, 70, 73
achievement history, 105
Adichie, Chimamanda Ngozi, 93, 95, 107
Adler-Kassner, Linda, 81, 88
Admissions Office, 82
Alsup, Janet, 34, 42
American College Testing (ACT), 84
An Evening with Friends of Second Language Writing, 106
Angelou, Maya, 91
applied linguistics, 5, 10, 13, 24, 53–57, 61, 64, 67, 69, 72–73, 75–76, 79, 86
Atkinson, Dwight, 12, 16, 18, 20–22, 27, 29–30
audience, 30, 61, 70, 72, 74–77

Babcock, Linda, 94, 107
Bazerman, Charles, 55, 65
Beaufort, Anne, 77–78
Beiser, Frederick C., 21, 31
Belcher, Diane, 27, 31
Bergstrom, Carl T., 93, 107
*Bildung*, 21, 31
bilingual, 36–37, 54
Blanton, Linda L., 12, 20
Braine, George, 67, 78
Brazil, 81

Brookfield, Stephen D., 92, 107
Brown, Christopher M., 31, 92–93, 107

Cahill, Kevin M., 21, 31
capital, 5, 23, 27, 31
career, 41, 44, 50, 52, 56–57, 62–64, 66, 68, 76, 78, 82, 88, 91
Carnegie Medal, 91
Carson, Joan G., 10, 11, 48, 53
Casanave, Christine Pearson, 12, 31, 66–68, 78, 79, 98, 107
CCCC Second Language Writing Standing Group, 95
Center for International Education, 82
Chamcharatsri, Pisarn Bee, 33, 39, 42, 54, 74, 86–87, 89
charm, 101
China, 14, 81
Cho, Seonhee, 27, 31
Christie, Agatha, 90
Clance, Pauline R., 90–91, 93, 95–99, 101, 107–108, 110
cognitive apprenticeship, 27
comfort zone, 104
competence, 28, 90, 101–103
composition studies (*see also* writing studies), 6, 11–13, 18, 36, 42, 55, 58, 59, 63, 67, 75, 77, 79
conference, 24, 30, 50, 61, 63, 71–72, 74, 88, 92, 100
confidence, 77, 94–95, 97, 103–

115

104, 107, 109
coping skills, mechanisms, 92, 100–101, 104
Correll, Shelley J., 93, 107
course, 16, 24–25, 28, 29, 37, 39, 40, 45, 50, 58, 59, 60, 81–85
creative writing, 95
cross-disciplinary, 54–55, 79, 93
Crusan, Deborah, 20, 84, 88, 90, 100, 107

Dancy, Elon T., 92–93, 107
Davies, Laura, 81, 88
department, 34–35, 38–39, 40–41, 56–57, 59–61, 63–64, 80–81, 83, 85–87, 98
disciplinary development, 6–7, 12, 18
discursively constructed, 6
dissertation, 23, 29–30, 35, 39, 44, 63, 74–75
diversity, 18, 27, 31, 55, 57, 59, 74, 84
documentation, 41, 85
Donahue, Christiane, 68, 79, 87–88
Dowell, Matt, 81, 88

editor, 16, 71, 74, 76, 77, 100
education, 6, 13, 20, 31, 36, 45, 51, 54–58, 61, 64, 69, 78, 79, 93, 96, 102, 107
Educational Psychology, 95
Elsevier Science Limited, 10
*ELT Journal*, 9
empirical methods, 9–10, 68, 70, 72–73
English Language Institute (ELI), 82
ESL: adult, 37
ESL Institute, 57–58
ESL Writing Program, 80–81
ESL, Director of, 81, 85

*ESP Journal*, 9
Evans, Nicholas, 27, 31

Facebook, 8, 24, 91
faculty, 22–23, 26, 28, 30, 33, 34–37, 39, 41–49, 54–57, 59, 60–64, 82–87, 92–94, 97, 107
failing,, 103
Ferris, Dana, 11–12
flagship journal, 3, 6, 18
Fleck, Ludwig, 30–31
Fraud Syndrome (see Impostor Syndrome), 90
Frost, Alanna, 81, 88

Garcia, Mike, 81, 88
Geertz, Clifford, 21, 31
Gelfand, Michele, 94, 107
genius, 32, 102–103
genre, 14–15, 51, 63
Germany, 81, 91
Gladwell, Malcolm, 25–26, 31
Google Scholar, 9
graduate school, 21–22, 31, 100
graduate student, 3, 8, 14–15, 24, 28, 34–40, 42, 58–59, 62–63, 66, 79–82, 87, 97, 106
grammar, 56, 60
grant, 34, 46, 56, 62, 101, 104
Groom, Nicholas, 50, 53
group solidarity, 48
Gunner, Jeanne, 87–88

Halliday, Michael, 29, 31
Hanauer, David, 35, 51, 53
Harklau, Linda, 76, 79
History, 95
Holliday, Adrian, 49, 53
Horner, Bruce, 79
Hunter, Rik, 81, 88
Hutchins, Holly M., 92, 107
Hyland, Ken, 12, 68, 77, 79

Index 117

identity (scholarly), 25, 33, 42, 61
identity construction, 36, 39
Iida, Atsushi, 44, 51, 53, 86–87, 89
Imes, Suzanne, 90–91, 93, 95, 98, 101, 107
Imposter Phenomenon Quiz, 95–97
Imposter Syndrome, 90–93, 95–101, 103, 106–107, 110
institution, 35, 37, 39, 41, 44–47, 49, 51, 54, 57, 62, 68, 75, 80–85
interdisciplinarity, 20, 33–34, 36, 41–43, 55–56, 61, 64–65, 76
International English Language Testing System (IELTS), 84
International Monetary Fund, 91
international students, 10, 37, 40, 62, 81, 84–85
international visa students, 37
Introduction, Methodology, Results, Analysis, Discussion (IMRAD), 76

Jacobs, Dale, 42
Jacquet, Jennifer, 93, 107
JAI Press, 10
Japan Association of College English Teachers, 52
Japanese public university, 44
Japanese teachers of English, 49
jargon, 5–6, 11, 14–15
Jeffery, Jill, 41
job insecurity, 47, 52
Johanek, Cindy, 67, 79
joint appointment, 33–36, 40–42, 54
journal, 3–4, 7, 10–19, 69, 70–72, 77
journal article, 27, 61–62, 70
*Journal of Basic Writing*, 9
*Journal of Response to Writing*, 19

*Journal of Second Language Writing* (JSLW), 3, 6–8, 10–20, 30–31, 43, 53, 65, 78; disciplinary dialogue, 16, 19, 20
journal reviewer, 69–72, 75, 77–78
junior faculty member, 50, 88
junior scholar, 66

K-12, 37, 54, 58, 64
Kanno, Yasuko, 76, 79
Kaplan, Robert B., 8, 9, 20, 30
Kay, Katty, 90, 93–95, 98–99, 103, 107
Kellejian, Kristine, 81, 88
Kim, Soo Hyon, 54, 86–87, 89
King, Molly M., 93, 107
knowledge-injection system, 27
Krishnan, Armin, 4, 20
Kubota, Ryuko, 48, 53, 55–65

Lagarde, Christine, 91
*Language Learning (Journal)*, 9, 20
Language Testing, 95
Language Testing Research and Practice, 95
Lave, Jean, 36, 43
Lee, Icy, 11–12, 24, 67
Leki, Ilona, 4, 10, 67, 79, 81
Levinson, Stephen C., 27, 31
linguistic minority, 76
linguistics, 8, 54, 56–58, 60, 62, 65, 67, 76, 81
literacy, 12, 20, 31, 51, 64, 76
Lu, Min-Zhan, 79

male, 94, 96–97
Manchón, Rosa, 12
manuscript, 4, 7, 15–16, 18, 62, 72, 77, 87, 107
Massachusetts Institute of Technology, 94
Matsuda, Paul Kei, 12, 19–20, 24, 27, 29, 31, 33, 36–37, 41, 43,

55, 65–66, 79, 105
McIntosh, Kyle, 89
memorandum of understanding (MOU), 39
mentoring, 35, 70–72, 75, 85–86, 92, 106
Merkel, Angela, 91
Miami University, 105
Micciche, Laura, 42
Middlebury Bread Loaf Writers' Conference, 97
Milton, John, 60
Mishler, Elliot, 28, 31
Mixed Methods International Research Association, 61
*Modern Language Journal*, 67, 79
Mueller, Derek, 81, 88

narrative, 8, 18, 31, 41–42, 74–75, 77, 87, 98
National Council of Teachers of English (NCTE), 62
National Endowment of the Humanities Summer Institute, 97
native-English speaker, 46, 49, 72
negotiation, 33, 35, 39, 48, 50, 52, 55, 61, 94
networking, 24, 51, 77, 87
non-native English speaker (NNES), 72
novice, 49, 56, 63, 70, 73, 76, 89

Ohmann, Richard, 5, 18, 20
Ortmeier-Hooper, Christina, 20

Pantelides, Kate, 81, 88
Peck-MacDonald, Susan, 31
Pelaez-Morales, Carolina, 89
person of color, 97
personal narrative, 70, 72, 77
placement test, 46, 81, 8–85, 87–89
poetry, 51, 53
practicum, 81
*Prairie Schooner*, 97
procrastination, 100–101
productivity, 41, 50
profession, 5, 8, 18, 20, 28, 62–63
professional development, 21, 23, 29, 45, 50, 52, 58, 63–64, 92–93
professional identity, 4, 12, 22, 25, 64
professional writing, 36
professionalization, 3–4, 6–7, 10, 15, 80
publishing, 4, 7, 9–14, 34, 46, 49, 60, 66–69, 71–72, 74, 76–78, 86
Purdue University, 105

Qualtrics, 95

rank, 14, 47, 83
*Reading and Rhetoric*, 9
relationship, 18, 20, 31, 47–48, 77, 92, 106
renewable contract position, 44
research, 3, 6–23, 26–35, 39, 41–53, 55, 57, 59–64, 67–69, 72–73, 78–88, 93, 105
research agenda, 42, 51, 61
research narratives, 61
resident multilingual, 75
resubmit, 73, 101
rhetoric and composition, 54, 64, 70, 72, 74, 79, 87
rigor, 6, 17, 19
Ritzer, George, 5, 20
Roche, Joyce, 91
Roen, Duane, 80, 82
Rose, Shirley K, 87–88, 110
Royster, Jacqueline Jones, 79
Ruecker, Todd, 20, 62, 66, 86–87, 89

# Index

rugged individualist, 103

Saenkhum, Tanita, 39, 54, 80–81, 86–89
salary, 93, 94
Santos, Terry, 10–11, 20
Saudi Arabia, 81
Schegloff, Emanuel, 24, 31
scholarly development, 21
scholarship, 8, 11–12, 14, 16, 18, 22, 29–30, 36–44, 52, 56, 59, 61, 78, 87
Scholastic Aptitude Test (SAT), 84
second language (L2), 3–18, 20, 25, 28, 33, 36–39, 41–47, 50–70, 74, 76–89, 106
second language acquisition (SLA), 6, 14, 16, 18, 37, 54
Second Language Research Forum (SLRF), 62
second language studies, 12, 13, 59
second language writers (graduate), 82
*Second Language Writing* (collection by Ilona Leki & Barbara Kroll), 3, 7, 9–10, 13, 20–21, 44, 57, 58, 66, 92, 95
second language writing, instructors, 81; transdisciplinary nature of, 37, 55–59, 62–64, 68–69, 73, 78
self-citation, 93, 107
self-esteem, 49–50, 99
service, 34–35, 39–41, 45–52, 56–57, 62–64, 84, 87
Sewanee Writers' Conference, 97
Sherman, Rose O., 104, 108
Shipman, Claire, 90, 93–95, 98–99, 103, 107
Shneider Model of Disciplinary Development: Stage Four, 18; Stage One, 8, 13; Stage Three, 12–13, 18; Stage Two, 9, 12, 16

Shneider, Alexander M., 6–9, 12–13, 18, 20
Shuck, Gail, 86, 89
Silva, Tony, 4, 9, 10, 19–20, 24, 67, 79, 89
Simpson, Steve, 20, 27, 31
Small, Deborah, 94, 107
Smith, Chris, 34, 39, 43
social development, 4, 6, 14, 31, 48, 52, 95, 98, 101, 104
social harmony, 48
Social Work, 95
Sociology, 95
South Korea, 81
standardized test scores, 84, 85
Stayn, Heidi, 94, 107
Storch, Neomy, 12
Streep, Meryl, 91
struggle, 53, 99, 100, 106
success, 19, 31, 41, 48, 87, 90–92, 96–98, 102, 104, 107–109
Superwoman/man/student, 103
support group, 104, 107
Swales, John, 27, 32
Symposium on Second Language Writing (SSLW), 19, 24, 41, 64, 86, 89, 105, 107

Taiwan, 81
Tardy, Christine M., 3, 20, 24, 41
teaching assistant, 38, 39, 58, 81, 86
Teaching English to Speakers of Other Languages (TESOL), 5, 9–13, 19–20, 30, 36–39, 53–64, 69, 81, 88, 95, 106
technology, 27–28, 45
tenure, 34–41, 53, 57, 60–61, 68, 73–74, 80, 84–88, 93, 105; case, 60–61, 84, 86; home, 34–35, 74; pre-, 39, 80–84, 88; untenured, 92
tenure and promotion, 34–35,

39–41, 60, 88, 105
tenure-track, 34–35, 41, 44, 53, 80–85, 88
TESOL International Association, 63
*TESOL Quarterly*, 9, 13, 19–20, 30, 53
TESOL Second Language Writing Interest Section, 95
Test of English as a Foreign Language (TOEFL), 84–85
Thailand, 81
transitions, 41, 58–59, 64, 75
translingual, 20, 79
Trimbur, John, 79

U.S. resident ESL students, 38
United States Institution of Higher Education, 80
University of New Hampshire (UNH), 56–61
University of New Mexico (UNM), 35, 37, 40, 73–74

Vandrick, Stephanie, 66–67, 78–79
volunteer, 63

von Humboldt, Wilhelm, 21, 31

Watson, Peter, 21, 32
Weber, Max, 4, 5, 20
Weiser, Irwin, 87–88
Wenger, Etienne, 25, 30, 32, 36, 43
West, Jevin D., 93, 107
Widdowson, Henry, 55, 65
Widnall, Sheila, 94
Williams, Raymond, 21, 32
Winslet, Kate, 91
Wittgenstein, Ludwig, 21, 30–32
World Englishes, 9, 72
*World Englishes* (Journal), 9, 72
Wright State University, 105
writing across communities (WAC), 36
writing program administrators (WPAs), 38, 80, 82, 84, 86–89
writing studies, 5, 13, 20, 65, 68, 70, 79

Young, Valerie, 90–91, 93–94, 95, 98, 100–103, 105, 108

# About the Editors

**Paul Kei Matsuda** is Professor of English and Director of Second Language Writing at Arizona State University, where he works closely with doctoral students specializing in second language writing. He is co-founding chair of the Symposium on Second Language Writing and editor of the Parlor Press Series on Second Language Writing. He has also served as  the President of the American Association for Applied Linguistics. He has published widely on the history, definition and identity of the field of second language writing and on topics such as identity and voice in writing, intercultural rhetoric, language differences, and writing program administration.

**Sarah Elizabeth Snyder** is a PhD Candidate at Arizona State University where she specializes in second language writing and writing program administration. Sarah also served as the Associate Director of Second Language Writing at ASU. Informed by the study of second language acquisition, sociolinguistics, and rhetoric and composition, her research areas concern the intersections of second language writing and writing program assessment. She is active in national organizations such as the  Symposium on Second Language Writing as well as the Council of Writing Program Administrators and their Graduate Organization, for which she has facilitated multiple mentoring and professional development events.

**Katherine Daily O'Meara** is Assistant Professor of Rhetoric and Composition and the Director of Composition at Emporia State University. Her major areas of interest include second language writing, writing program administration, rhetoric and composition/writing studies, L1 and L2 teacher training and professional development, institutional ethnography, first-year writing, and threshold concepts. Kat is an active member of the Council of Writing Program Administrators and is the outgoing Past Chair of the WPA-GO, the CWPA graduate organization. She delights in teaching and mentoring graduate and undergraduate students in English, yoga, craft beers, and her two cats.

www.ingramcontent.com/pod-product-compliance
Lightning Source LLC
Chambersburg PA
CBHW021859230426
43671CB00006B/454